CAMPUS GODS ON TRIAL

OTHER BOOKS BY THE SAME AUTHOR

LITERARY CRITICISM
   C. S. Lewis: Apostle to the Skeptics
SOCIAL THEORY
   Early Christians of the 21st Century
POETRY
   The Factual Dark
BASIC THEOLOGY
   Stop Looking and Listen

CAMPUS GODS
ON TRIAL

BY CHAD WALSH

THE MACMILLAN COMPANY
New York   1956

For Viola B. Tuttle

And in memory of Charles A. Tuttle

You Athenians are very religious, I can see that. While I was on my way here, I had a look at the things you worship, and I even came on an altar with this inscription: 'To an *unknown* God.' As if you didn't have a long enough list of Gods already! But I'm going to tell you about this unknown God. . . .

—*Paul's remarks to the Athenians (slightly expanded)*

ACKNOWLEDGMENTS

THIS BOOK GREW OUT OF A MAGAZINE ARTICLE, "COLLEGE Students Are from Missouri," in *Presbyterian Life*, September 16, 1950. The editors have kindly given me permission to incorporate large parts of the article in various sections of the present work.

For very painstaking and intelligent criticism of the manuscript in its early stages, I am indebted to my wife, Eva, and to my good friends Robert and Jacqueline Jackson, Carroll E. Simcox, and Robert H. Glauber. They helped me clarify the thought and expression more than I can well say.

A great many other friends, through correspondence and personal conversations, assisted me in the formative period of the book. I list those that come to mind: Edwin E. Aubrey, Paul M. Bechtel, John Gilland Brunini, Henry Brevoort Cannon, Edward T. Dell, Harry Jones, Wilber Katz, Alwin Louden, David Maitland, John Mulder, Chomingwen Pond, Carl E. Purinton, Alfred Reimers, Alexander and Janet Smith, Marjorie Kurfman Sneller, David Wesley Soper, Harry Taylor, Hyatt H. Waggoner, J. Rodman Williams, George P. Winship, Jr.

I know that many other names should be listed. In a very real sense, this book is a composite labor, though the responsibility for its shortcomings, as well as its particular emphases, must be mine alone.

I have mentioned none of my students at Beloit College; so many of them directly or indirectly aided and stimulated me that it would be ungracious to single out individual names. But I am deeply grateful to them, and to the students on other campuses who have also had a large share—larger than they can realize—in enriching my understanding of the campus and its gods.

CONTENTS

WHY THIS BOOK WAS WRITTEN

A GREAT DEAL OF NONSENSE IS TALKED AND WRITTEN about "our godless campuses." The campuses are not godless at all. They are overpopulated with gods. The gods lurch against you as you walk from building to building; they keep you company in the student union, and they attend classroom lectures with you.

Some of the favorite classroom gods are Progress, Relativism, Scientism, and Humanitarianism. Each of them embodies a great deal of truth. But the trouble is, none of these gods is big enough. If you try to follow one of them exclusively, he will let you down flat on your face. And if you combine them, they start a civil war inside your head.

To make things still more complicated, there are the national gods. They do not need any classroom propaganda, for they are already worshiped in every state of the Union. The most important one is Materialism—the pursuit of the dollar sign. When a recent commencement speaker at an illustrious eastern college expounded the spiritual importance of getting rich as quickly and thoroughly as possible, he was echoing the religion preached in magazine advertisements and the output of Hollywood.

But the "million dollars in a hurry" creed is less noticeable on the campus than a few decades ago. The Depression of the 1930's, when many once prosperous citizens found themselves selling apples at street corners, helped to tone it down and develop a humbler form of Materialism, whose god is Security. Most students today do not aspire to a million dollars. They want to train themselves for a safe niche in a well established business firm, and retire on an adequate pension at the age of sixty-five.

One other God must be mentioned. He is the God whose activities are described in the Bible.

The relation between this God and the rival deities—Scientism, Relativism, and the rest—varies greatly from campus to campus. In some places, he has an even break. There is a Department of Religion, staffed by men the academic and intellectual equals of the professors who teach physics and sociology. Scattered through the various departments are Christian instructors who are not reluctant to stand up for their beliefs when anyone buttonholes them and asks questions. There may even be a college chapel, with a competent chaplain, and a network of student religious organizations. Such a campus offers the student a chance to make his own study of comparative religion. He can learn about *all* the available gods, not forgetting the one God, and come to his own conclusions.

But many colleges and universities—among them some of the most eminent—have stacked the cards. Either there is no Department of Religion, or it is a lame-duck affair, presided over by a superannuated clergyman of feeble academic attainments. Most of the departments are overwhelmingly manned by secularists of one sort or another, zealous in proclaiming their particular religions—only they don't use the word "religion."

It is true that secular campuses have a way of paying their nominal respects to "our spiritual heritage" by an annual binge called Religious Emphasis Week. Two or three preachers are summoned to give pep talks about the things of the spirit; the Drama Department presents a pageant on some safely nonsectarian religious theme, and there is a concert of sacred music.

Such affairs are an insult to the intelligence of students. I wonder what a college freshman, interested in chemistry, would say if the dean told him: "Of course we don't offer any classes in chemistry, but we'll be glad to bring a couple of chemists to the campus for a week every spring to satisfy your curiosity. We'll call it 'Chemical Emphasis Week.' "

One does not have to be a Christian to see the absurdity of the situation. Students, like everybody else, are looking for an answer, a God, big enough to encompass all partial answers and partial gods, and to help the latter work together as a team. Christianity aims to provide that answer and that God. But how can it be either accepted or rejected if nobody explains what it is?

Theology is as systematic and disciplined a study as geology or psychology. It is based on the observed facts of religious experience through the centuries. It has been worked out by some of the keenest minds that ever functioned. (One does not condescend to Augustine, Aquinas, Calvin, or Reinhold Niebuhr.) On the intellectual level it can hold its own with any other mental discipline.

Theology also happens to be the most practical of all studies. Composition 2 is useful for the person who wants to be a professional writer or prepare club reports; Farm Management 4 is intended for the future farm manager. But theology is useful for everybody. It deals with problems that are life-and-death matters for everyone, every day. You can put it to work all the time, not just keep it on the reference shelf for special occasions.

To deny a student access to so essential a tool of thought and everyday living is as great a crime against him as to remove one lobe of his brain.

In this book I want to do some things your college or university ought to be doing and probably isn't. First of all, I intend to put the rival campus gods on trial. I can see some good in all of the gods and am not recommending capital punishment; but I also see some positive evil in all of them but One.

I do not pretend to be a neutral bystander. I have served most of the available gods at one time or another, and have come to believe that only One of them can be completely depended upon. For this reason, I shall devote special attention to Christianity, and shall try to show what it *is*, and also (just as important) what it *isn't*. While doing this I hope to take up the most common stumbling blocks, both intellectual and emotional, that lurk between Christianity and anyone looking at it from the outside.

Whatever god you may choose, the choice will be the major turning point of your life. It is more important even than entering college, embarking on a career, or getting married.

The god or God that you select will go to work and remake you in his image. After serving your particular deity for twenty years you will be a very different person. *Ideas Have Consequences* is the title of a book that came out some time ago. Gods have still greater and more permanent consequences —in you.

C. W.

BELOIT COLLEGE

I

THE FIERY FURNACE AND THE LUKEWARM BATH

IF YOU COME FROM A FIERY-FURNACE HOME, IT WAS dominated by religion. And the chances are that you didn't like it. God, usually pictured as a cosmic policeman, was the invisible guest at every meal; His name was invoked to keep you from doing the things you wanted to do; He seemed the private Gestapo of your parents.

Perhaps "fiery furnace" isn't the best title. "Overhanging glacier" is the way it often appears. Christianity and its God are a remorseless force, slowly grinding the joy out of life. In the church down the street the terrors of hell are weekly proclaimed; the evils of dancing, card playing, even movie going and mixed swimming are denounced as vehemently as if Moses had forbidden them. And the theology is likely to be "the Bible from cover to cover," which in extreme cases is taken to mean that the world was created six thousand years ago (no matter what the geologists may claim), and that Adam and Eve are historical figures as certain as Franklin Delano Roosevelt.

Fiery-furnace homes are the background of a small minority of students in most colleges and universities. But they breed a consistently high percentage of rebels. Part of the rebellion is emotional. It is directed against a drab puritanism. As one student put it:*

I do not understand why the ——— Church thinks that dancing and card playing are sinful. I know a young girl, who, in order to teach Sunday school, had to sign a promise that she would not dance as long as she taught. Why should she have to give up a perfectly innocent thing like dancing, because she started teaching Sunday school?

No wonder that the fiery-furnace home produces the typical campus rebel, who signs his declaration of independence by outcarousing his fellow students. The revolt of the emotions is powerfully reinforced by the uprising of the intellect; the acids of science in the biology and geology labs eat away the rigid theology of childhood.

Many vehement agnostics emerge at the end of the four years. The only kind of Christianity they have personally experienced is the fiery furnace. When it is discredited, a vacuum is left, to be filled by one of the campus gods—the Gospel of Progress, the Gospel of Money-Making, Humanitarianism, or just plain Eat, Drink, and Be Merry.

Much more numerous are the students who know religion only as a lukewarm bath. Probably a majority come from such homes. The parents maintain a nominal church connection, and hustle the children off to Sunday school. And that is about all. Mother and Father frequently choose to relish the Sunday

* For the source of the student comments quoted throughout this book, see Appendix A.

morning tranquillity by lingering over the second cup of coffee and the fat Sunday paper. When Christianity is talked about—which is not often—it seems indistinguishable from a vague humanitarianism and the duties of citizenship. Reduced to a poetic edition of ethical culture, it has about as much driving power.

A lukewarm-bath student, coming to Maplecrest College or Gargantua University, discovers (on the great majority of campuses, at least) that the prevailing religious tone is polite skepticism or mild indifference. His religion is already a pallid thing; it becomes more so. He may indeed retain and develop whatever idealism he has inherited from his Sunday school and church, but it finds newer and more exciting outlets. Suspecting that his family's religion is merely a prettified version of common-sense ethics, and unacquainted with any sturdier brand of Christianity, he turns to one of the secular faiths, and finds there a god whom he can honestly worship.

A fortunate minority of students come from warm-fire homes. Christianity is so much a part of the family's daily living that you could pay them a visit and not be able to put the difference into words, except to say that there was something spontaneous, joyous, and outreaching in the atmosphere. Investigating further, you would find that the parents and children go to church *together;* that God is a living friend, not a Gestapo chief; that the smallest children have been taught to pray as naturally as to reach for the peanut butter; that in a very quiet and unconscious way the family has gradually become a province of the universal Church.

In such homes, God is so real that there seems to be no necessity to speculate over the age of the earth or the exact way that the Hebrews crossed the Red Sea; but, because God is real, the family is not tempted to go to the opposite extreme and reduce Christianity to a lukewarm set of moral platitudes.

A warm-fire student has relatively few religious difficulties when he reaches the campus. The curt questions of his agnostic friends will, of course, compel him to think through the theology that he has unconsciously assumed, and bring it up to a seventeen-year-old level. But this is not too difficult, because he doesn't have much to unlearn. His main problem is often this: to some extent he has lived in the reflected warmth of the whole family's religious life, and his own share may be a bit secondhand. Now that he is on his own, he no longer has the warm fire of home to keep him from getting chilly; he must create his own fire as he goes along.

Perhaps a fourth class of homes should be added. These are a small minority, but an important one. I am thinking of homes where the parents are stanch agnostics or atheists. At one time agnosticism was an exciting thing. Today it has hardened into a new orthodoxy, and become staid and respectable. This standardized and somewhat smug unbelief dominates a number of homes especially in urban areas; and in such homes the parents usually fancy themselves as intellectuals. Children of such parents are militantly kept away from churches and Sunday schools. They go to college innocent of any direct knowledge of Christianity.

On the campus they find an attitude not too different from that they have left behind. So for them there is no conflict between the old home and the new one, and they usually drift along for some time, without giving religion much thought. In a few cases, however, when they are engaged in a complete rebellion against the folks back home, their revolt leads them in the direction of religion. Tense family situations sometimes arise when children of agnostics insist on being baptized after they reach college.

Regardless of what kind of home a student comes from, he is likely to know exceeding little of formal theology and the way it is related to everything he will learn at college. He is a victim of buck passing. The public schools say, "The Supreme Court won't let us talk about religion." Parents toss the ball to the churches. The churches cram what instruction they can into one hour on Sunday morning, with makeshift equipment and amid general confusion. The result is a blurred jumble of half-facts and half-truths, none of which will stand up well to a probing attack by a committed atheist. Let me cite two case histories. The first is a boy:

Every Sunday morning until I went to high school, my parents dragged me out of bed and sent me to Sunday school. When I got there I would play with friends through a sermon and then continue my play through a class. When I graduated from the eighth grade I was confirmed in the Church. I had no more idea of what happened to me than I did of atomic physics.

Here are a girl's reminiscences:

From the time I was two years old until I came to college I went to Sunday school every Sunday, rain or shine. I started going to church regularly when I was confirmed as an eighth grader in grade school. I taught the nursery department during my last two years in high school, taught a class of the Bible School our church sponsors during the summer vacation. . . . With all this religious background, one would think I would know something about my religion. But I don't! . . . All the facts I've learned in Sunday school, and heard in church and religious meetings, are in such a garbled state in my mind that if someone should ask me to explain my religion or what Christianity is, I shouldn't be able to give an intelligent reply.

These two quotations explain why most bull sessions on religion are so unproductive. To share one's ignorance with other ignorant people is good fellowship, but not necessarily enlightening. Before arguing the merits of Christianity or how it should be applied to the atom bomb, labor unions, and progressive education, one needs to know what Christianity actually is.

Another thing should be added to all this. The religious background of a student obviously has a very important effect on the particular religious problems he will meet on the campus. But something equally crucial is his general frame of mind as he packs his suitcase and heads for Maplecrest or Gargantua.

Occasionally he goes as a colonist from the old country, determined to transplant his old way of life onto the campus. He carries with him Daddy's political views and Mother's code of polite behavior, and is unwilling to budge an inch in his loyalty to them. Such a student, naturally enough, takes along his particular brand of religion, if any, and fiercely protects it together with all the other heirlooms of his life back home.

At the opposite extreme is the student who arrives on the campus in revolt against everything in general. In most cases, some sort of religion—however harmless and insipid—has existed back home. So one part of his total rebellion is to chuck over religion, together with maternal precepts about the way nice young people behave, and Father's advice as to the choice of a career. Once arrived on the campus, he extends the rebellion by a running battle with deans, house mothers, and professors. If the tone of the campus is on the atheistic side, such a student may find himself in a quandary: whether to revolt against his parents' religion or against his alma mater's atheism. But usually there is enough vague religion on the campus, which can be identified with religion back home, to justify the continuing revolt against all traditional faiths.

However, the largest contingent of entering freshmen are those who are in revolt against the old home because they want a new and roomier one. They are not rebels by nature, but they feel cramped in the little house where they grew up. If the campus can provide them with a more spacious home, fine! They are then quite willing to learn its customs and taboos and abide by them. Therefore, if the old home was religious, and the new home—the campus—is skeptical, skepticism becomes one clause of the naturalization papers.

Except for the handful of students who try to transplant the old country when they reach the campus, the four years of college are a war of liberation, waged against the entire world or against home and the home town. This is a very good thing, even if it means sleepless nights for the parents. A student comes to college hoping to discover that hidden core of individuality, the mysterious "I" which makes him different from more than two billion other "I's." And he is trying to decide what he will do with that "I" after he finds it: how he will train it and direct it, so that it will become what he wants it to be thirty years from now.

That is what college is mainly about. And the quest of the secret "I" is inextricably linked with the search for a more spacious home, where that "I" will have sufficient room to grow. The campus is such a home. It offers a new family, bigger and more exciting. We shall need to examine some of the family customs and cliques.

2

WEEK ENDS WITH THE ZETES, DAYS IN CLASS

IF THE COLLEGE IS SMALL ENOUGH IT MAY BE A FRIENDLY and satisfying family in itself. The students do things en masse: go to football games 90 per cent strong, bellow out college songs whenever anyone suggests it, and speak the name of Maplecrest as small children murmur the word Mamma.

But most colleges and universities are too large for this. The school is an institution which impersonally mails out grades at the end of each semester or quarter, serves ultimatums from the offices of the deans, and collects tuition fees.

Cliques or subfamilies naturally grow up. Some of them center around favorite activities. The local actors have their own jargon and hangouts; athletes gang together; intellectuals meet in small groups to converse about Kafka, Sartre, or whoever is the esoteric figure of the moment.

On most campuses, though, the really weighty subfamilies are the fraternities and sororities. Like the family back home, they are a bewildering mixture of good and bad. But that isn't the point. For many students they are the flaming center of loyalty. Long after Maplecrest College or Gargantua University has faded into a comfortably vague memory, you will find the old grads coming back to visit the Zeta Zeta Zetas (called the Zetes); frequently they set foot on no other part of the campus.

A fraternity is a cozy place because not everybody belongs to it. We all enjoy the feeling of being part of an "in-group." The old family was such a group; the fraternity is its campus equivalent. You can't be an insider unless there are outsiders.

Where the old family leaves off, the new family takes over. One of its main missions is to guide and systematize the war of liberation against the home town and the home folks, and therefore it exercises a control that would have been intolerable at the hands of parents. This phenomenon is common to all revolutionary movements. The citizens of France clamored for the right to serve in Napoleon's disciplined army and carry forward the work of Revolution; the modern Communist, considering himself as a rebel, submits to a discipline more rigid than that of the assembly-line worker for Chrysler or Ford.

The fraternity or sorority nurtures rebellion, freedom, and nonconformity of a strictly specified kind. The new member had once been told by Mother when to wear a necktie; now his fraternity brothers inform him when he must wear a tuxedo. (But the tuxedo is also a symbol of the new freedom!) Many a girl who has resented her mother's attempt to steer her toward "nice boys," meekly acquiesces when her sorority sisters indicate to her which fraternities are desirable sources for dates. Nonetheless, all this is growth in freedom. Discipline voluntarily accepted is not the same as discipline unwillingly inherited.

One big advantage of a fraternity is that it helps its members get into trouble and then helps them get out again. Although coming home pie-eyed and sick is not a good thing in itself, it can have good consequences if it leads you to investigate your own soul for the first time. And if you are going to get into trouble it is sensible to do it under controlled conditions, so that the results will fall short of catastrophe.

Consider the new fraternity man who tries to keep up with his brothers. They have had more basic training. About one o'clock in the morning he quietly passes out under a table at the Green Hutch. His companions contritely lead him into the car and drive back to the house, where they carefully tuck him into bed.

Perhaps he has always thought of himself as a self-possessed young man who has the situation under control, morning, noon, and night. He knows better now. Plain experience has taught him that his self-possession is a frail thing, at the mercy of a few slugs of alcohol. After the fourth drink he is ready to deliver public orations in front of the frat house or call up the Dean and tell him a dirty joke. Man, it appears, is a rational animal only under optimum conditions.

A hang-over turns a man into a philosopher in still another way. It compels him to ask some of the right questions. If a beast takes possession during a bout with alcohol, what is normally in possession? Is it the mysterious "I" which now shines more brightly because it can be so easily eclipsed by a little strong drink? And what is pleasure, and what is pain? Can you have one without the other? Can life be lived primarily for pleasure, or does every kind of pleasure have its own sort of hang-over? Is there a hierarchy or pyramid of pleasures? Is it possible that sinking quietly beneath the table is not the apex of the pyramid?

Another lesson from the adventure is that man does not live alone. The freshman remembers vaguely, but with gratitude, that his brothers hustled him home and into bed, to save him from the local police; they also dissuaded him from giving an oration in front of the fraternity house, or calling up the Dean, though both ideas seemed very good at the time.

In addition to alcohol, there is sex. It is the favorite topic at bull sessions, and is a main plank of the new freedom. No matter how grim and vigilant deans and house mothers may be, they do not have the final decision and control. They can't be everywhere at once, and on most campuses the supervision is more casual than at home.

Very few students go through four years without falling in love once, or even more than once. They advance systematically, in conformity with local custom, through the graduated stages of going steady and necking and petting and pinning. At some point, usually an early one, they recognize the fire they are playing with. Shall they plunge in, or stand at the edge of the conflagration that lures them forward?

To be in love and feel the tidal pull of sexual yearning is an object lesson, even more powerful than alcohol and hangovers, of the old platitude that no action of any importance concerns only one person. Sex involves a minimum of two; and, at a slight remove, it touches a widening circle of parents, relatives, friends, and possibly lives not yet in the world.

Some students obey the stop sign, and some do not. The decision is not an easy one to make. No Moses has carved the laws of the new freedom on tablets of stone. Indeed, the gospel of liberty, as inculcated in the fraternities and sororities, turns out to be stronger on the negative than on the positive side. The one positive commandment is, "Whatever you do, don't be fool enough to get caught."

The campaign of liberation against Mother and Father is conducted with vigor and clarity of purpose, but no one is very sure how to use the resulting freedom. "Group opinion" is no guide when the chips are down. Everybody in the group is as confused as everybody else.

The greater the liberty achieved, the deeper the sense of uncertainty and confusion. "My friends go in circles," one student wrote. "They live mostly for the moment. They seldom dare to face the future without a grim outlook. They are afraid. They are afraid of life and death and illness and love and God and Christ."

To make the situation more difficult, the same confusion prevails in the classroom. Or, to put it more exactly, Professor A will give exceedingly definite answers, and Professor B in the next classroom will make replies equally assured—but they flatly contradict each other. Only the most naïve freshman can believe that all professors are united in an unshakable alliance, intent upon selling one unified set of ideas and attitudes to the students. A professor's greatest pride is his independence of thought; if too many of his colleagues agree with him about anything he begins to worry.

The strident and contradictory voices that issue from the classroom can be illustrated by looking at a relatively impersonal problem—war. Every college student is crucially concerned about war. Either he is likely to be put into a uniform, or (a girl) she fears for her boy friend.

Let's imagine a student during his first two or three years of college and follow him briefly through a number of his classes. He wants to find out why wars start, and how they can be prevented. It must be confessed in advance that there is a touch of caricature in our picture of his professors and their answers; but the exaggeration merely high-lights the prevailing confusion.

Our student takes Economics 11 as his one elective during

the first semester of the freshman year. Professor Carwell, famous for biting lectures and a sharp wit, explains war very simply. Wars break out because people want to make money. Two industrial nations get in a tangle over the exploitable markets of the Balkans, Asia, or Africa, and soon the Marines are called in.

This seems reasonable; but next semester the student elects Political Science 3 as a step toward working off the "distributional requirement in the social sciences." Professor Grumstark, whose bulging eyes cannot recognize any face more than three paces away, mumbles darkly that wars begin because of Wicked Men in High Places. A politician gets himself in a tight spot and starts a war in order to divert public attention from his incompetence.

This too seems reasonable; but our student, now a sophomore, signs up for Sociology 1. (B's are said to be plentiful in young Mr. Holmes's section.) Mr. Holmes, a neo-Malthusian, believes that people are having too many babies, and that wars start as an attempt to steal enough farmland to feed the extra mouths; but, unlike Professors Carwell and Grumstark, he offers a ray of hope. "Control of population increase," he half whispers toward the end of the semester.

By this time any student in quest of wisdom has a right to be more mystified than before he started. Our sophomore begins looking for an explanation that will tie all the explanations together. "Try psych," a friend suggests. "That's the really up-to-date stuff, if you want to know what makes people act the way they do."

Professor Drillingham turns out to be a psychologist of the more pessimistic school. When Mr. Holmes's solution to the problem of war is called to his attention, he smiles sadly and answers, "Too simple, too simple." Man is a bundle of "drives," he explains. One of these is the aggressive drive. Don't ask why it's there. It is. But can't something be done about it? Can't psychology itself provide techniques, methods for educating the drive out of people's make-up? A few psychologists entertain such hopes, Professor Drillingham concedes; but they are optimists. Utopians, utopians.

Another distributional requirement is partially fulfilled by English 13, The Development of English Literature, which gallops from Beowulf in translation to "The Love Song of J. Alfred Prufrock." It is immediately evident that English Literature has a great deal to do with war; the novelists, poets, and dramatists are always writing about it, though few of them bother to say what starts it or how to stop it. The same lack of philosophic concern is displayed by Professor Brunch, a hearty man of fifty-three, whose greatest pride is his summer mountain-climbing exploits in the Rockies. At times he smacks his lips with positive relish as immortal words (to be remembered for the final) depict the smashing of skulls, disemboweling of torsos, and cities rising upward in smoke. To him, war is an enormous stage setting, and a stimulus for heroes to be heroic, traitors to betray, and the plot to get under way.

Finally, in his junior year, our student elects Religion 21, hoping that it will give him a whole view of man. There he is firmly told that wars start because of "Original Sin," whatever that is. (Professor Perkins never quite finds time to define his terms.)

War is just one example. If you are looking for the final truth about the family (what it is, and what should be done about it), juvenile delinquency, socialized medicine, the United Nations, or the relative merits of Aristotle and Sartre, you will find the same thing. Each professor has his own pair of spectacles, and views the world through them. In fitting the jigsaw puzzle of life together, you will have to do most of the hard work yourself. The classrooms are the halls of Babel.

Then why go to college anyway? Not to get the pat or the ready-made answer, but to begin asking the important questions, and to learn how to think out a question for yourself, when the challenge stares you in the face.

3

MOSTLY ISMS

THE CLASSROOMS ARE THE HALLS OF BABEL. THE DORMS and frat houses are their annexes. But gradually, through all the din and smoke, a few gods begin to emerge. Most of them have names ending in -ism.

One important exception is Progress. Thirty years ago it would have been necessary to say much more about this deity than today. Once all-powerful, he is now battered and punch-drunk. Most of his disciples are middle-aged men who try to believe that everything reported in the newspapers since 1914 is a bad dream.

Progress means that things are getting better all the time. Usually it also implies that they can't help getting better. History is a roller coaster ride, always upward and onward.

The religion of Progress has two sturdy parents. One is the Judaeo-Christian tradition. Jews and Christians have always believed that history is moving toward something in particular; that at "the end of time," God himself will bring all things to perfection. This is a minority viewpoint. Most of humanity has agreed with the ancient Greeks and the Hindus that time is a meaningless illusion or at best an endlessly repeating cycle,

16

like a snake chasing its tail, so that Socrates drinks the hemlock one day and will drink it again and again as the wheel of time revolves back to the same point.

Now it is possible to forget about God, or push him off on a dead-end street, but retain—from force of habit—a stubborn conviction that history has meaning, that time has meaning, that both are moving forward, toward something definite and desirable.

Then, to this faith, add a strong dash of the theory of Evolution—the story of how life has gone places, and presumably is still on the march. From the amoeba to a professor of biology is impressive progress; but the professor himself may be only a way station toward some unimaginable future perfection. And modern democracy perhaps compares with ancient tyrannies as the utopian society of the future will compare with present-day democracy.

With two such vigorous parents—the Judaeo-Christian tradition and Evolution—the doctrine of Progress dominated popular thinking around the turn of the century. History seemed to be acting according to schedule. Slavery had been abolished almost everywhere; women were getting their rights; free and democratic governments were springing up in place of despotism; there were signs that war itself might be on the way out. Like a golden thread through the whole pattern of modern history, the scientists were hard at work, laying the technological foundations for the coming utopia.

The newspaper headlines since 1914 can be briefly summarized. One world war was fought. In its aftermath, the "inevitable" swing toward democracy and political freedom reversed itself: Germany and Italy went Fascist; Japan turned away from democratic experiments; Russia threw off a tsar and acquired a Lenin and a Stalin, plus a dictatorship that made the old tsar seem a feeble bungler; slavery, under other names, began to reappear in many countries.

There were still darker headlines in the newspapers: Buchenwald and Maidanek and Katyn Forest. Science itself became a kept woman in some countries, dominated and directed by dictators and party chiefs. And World War II was waged as much against women and children as against men in uniform. Its symbols are the concentration camp, the gas chamber, the block-buster, the incendiary bomb, and the A-bomb.

Progress is possible, but it isn't inevitable. It comes about when two conditions are present: (1) people are willing to work and sweat and use their brains; (2) they know where they want to go.

The second point needs a bit of amplification. When you talk about Progress, what do you really mean? Progress toward what? Take America today, and try to decide whether we are progressing. If the yardstick is the standard of living the index of real wages will give you one answer. But if you measure progress by the stability of family life the divorce statistics will suggest a different verdict. One main weakness of Progress as a religion is that the worshipers are men who walk into a railroad station and say to the clerk at the window, "Give me a ticket to some place," and then hopefully board the train, without looking at the ticket.

The real danger today is not that people will naïvely worship Progress, but that they will erect altars to Despair. This deity already has his disciples on the campus. One girl expressed it concisely:

In this day and age some of my friends feel it's impossible to accept Christianity, being kind and a brother to all men, without being knifed in the back. The world is too rotten for even the power of Christianity to save it.

And a boy drew these practical conclusions:

I find it hard to be a Christian in a world so completely filled with uncertainty. The conditions that influence my early life are such that I shall never know how much time there is left or what the future may bring. As a result, I find myself saying, "To hell with everything and everybody. Live fast, free, and furiously; the devil take the hindmost, I'm going to have fun."

However, there is a better god than either Progress or Despair, and he attracts many students who are impatient of futile speculation about the future. They want to be doing something useful now, and let the future take care of itself. Their religion is Humanitarianism.

Humanitarianism means being kind to other people, helping them in any way you can, working for an improvement in social conditions.

There is little that need be said about Humanitarianism, for there is nothing to be said against it, and everything for it. Humanitarianism is simply the second half—"Thou shalt love thy neighbor as thyself"—of the Great Commandment given by Christ, when asked to summarize the moral law.

Humanitarianism didn't just spring up spontaneously in the human heart. The ancient Romans had hospitals, but these were strictly on a pay-as-you-go basis. The American visitor to certain parts of Asia is shocked by how little social spirit he finds. People look out for their families and close friends, and call it quits. Christ gave the word "neighbor" a steadily widening meaning, and Humanitarianism has cherished and applied that meaning, but often forgotten the source. How long the second half of the Great Commandment will be obeyed if the first half is neglected ("Thou shalt love the Lord thy God with all thy heart, and with all thy soul, and with all thy mind") is a question that cannot be evaded. Flowers grow best in soil that offers rich food for their roots. But all praise and honor to Humanitarianism—as long as it lasts and as far as it goes.

One postscript. "Humanitarianism" is a word that should be used only when the motive is outgoing love and a desire to help other people without expecting anything in return. Often what appears to have this motivation is really a refined form of selfishness. The genuine humanitarian supported the Marshall Plan and the Point Four Program because they were ways in which America could share some of its abundance with other nations, and help them get on their feet. The pseudohumanitarian coldly decided that it was worth a few billions to buy the friendship of various countries, and keep them on our side of the Iron Curtain.

Perhaps motivation seems unimportant. The help given is real in any case; but there is a parting of the ways when circumstances change and kindness no longer pays off in tangible rewards. Then the pseudohumanitarian will pull out, and the real humanitarian (with love in his heart) will hang on.

Among the other gods with names ending in -ism, Americanism is frequently advocated but turns out to be slippery and elusive. If you asked each of our ninety-six Senators to write a 500-word theme on Americanism, you would find that half a dozen deities masquerade under one name. To many people, Americanism means, "Give business its head, and keep the men in Washington under control"; to others, it implies the welfare state, benevolently directed from Washington.

To some enthusiasts, Americanism—whatever it means— is a total way of life: patriotism, philosophy, and religion all in one wrapper. In that case it is a tribal faith, comparable to Japanese Shinto.

But Americanism at its noblest stands for several splendid

things: democratic government, civil liberties, the right of a man to be a good citizen and at the same time seek and worship a God who is more than a magnified Uncle Sam. Real Americanism is not a religion but a framework within which everyone is free to choose and serve his own religion. As long as we keep it that way, Americanism will be a trustworthy servant, not a straitjacket nor an idol.

Once in a while Capitalism is extolled in language fit only for religious devotions, though commonly the worshipers prefer the name Free Enterprise for their deity. Even less needs to be said here. Capitalism is a particular economic system. It has nothing to say about beauty, love, and God. The most rugged capitalist, when he comes home, hangs up his silk hat and plays with his children or makes love to his wife like everybody else. So, whether or not you think Capitalism is the best way of regulating production and commerce, it is not built to regulate that hidden "I" which you are in the process of discovering.

Communism,* the last of the divine isms to be considered here, makes far more sweeping claims. It takes the idea of "economic man" (already developed by the capitalist economists) and says that art, philosophy, social customs, thought itself, are by-products of "who produces what and gets what from whom." Therefore, if you radically reconstruct the economic system—say, by doing away with private property—you can remake the face of the earth so that a terrestrial paradise, called the Classless Society, will gradually come into be-

* Communism must be sharply distinguished from Socialism. The Socialist movement, as it has developed in America and western Europe, is as much Christian as Marxist in its origin and leadership, and displays a respect for the individual and his rights which is completely lacking in Communism.

ing. And Communism adds that history is inexorably moving in that direction. You can't stop history; the wise thing is to jump on its bandwagon.

In fact, Communism is a highly sophisticated version of the gospel of inevitable Progress, and the only form of that faith with much vitality today. It has the advantage of knowing what destination is printed on the railroad ticket, and its theory of dialectical materialism provides the faithful with a pair of binoculars by which they can study the social evolution of the cave man and peer also into the classless future. There is food for both the mind and the heart. No wonder, then, that Communism has in effect become a religion wherever it is dominant. You could set up a whole series of parallels between Russian Communism and Christianity:

COMMUNISM	CHRISTIANITY
Writings of Marx, Lenin, Stalin	Bible
Communist party	Priesthood
Proletariat	Church
Private property	Original sin
Classless society	Kingdom of God
Withering away of the state	Second coming of Christ

The body of Lenin is revered like the relics of saints; the vast demonstrations in Red Square are equivalent to the more elaborate rituals of formal religion.

Marx himself was a very religious kind of atheist. He inherited the fierce passion against social injustice bequeathed by Micah and some other Old Testament prophets, and he derived from both Christianity and Judaism (perhaps quite unconsciously) the conviction that history is moving somewhere in particular.

The passion for social justice is the good thing in Marxism. But it has two defects which are sufficient to turn it into a nightmare like George Orwell's *Nineteen Eighty-four*, once it gets into full power anywhere.

The first of these fundamental defects is the belief that if you create the right economic system all evils will take care of themselves. Specifically, the Marxists tend to regard private control of property as the prime source of everything wrong with society. But the root of evil lies deeper—in the human heart. Monks in a monastery, practicing their religious communism, can still be backbiters, schemers, and exploiters of one another in subtle ways. The children on a playground have no bank accounts, no property vested in their names; yet for cruelty, and general nastiness, they can rival anybody. Observe how they struggle for prestige, and how mercilessly they will gang up on one unfortunate. The playground can be a jungle.

In capitalism, private property is an instrument through which human meanness can express itself. If the state takes over the property, then the state becomes the instrument of meanness. To achieve any fundamental improvement, you have to get at the elemental meanness itself—in the heart. And that is what the real religions attempt to do.

The other fatal defect of Marxism is that it regards man as nothing but a very highly developed animal. This is the logical implication of atheism, and the Marxists are very logical. If man is merely an animal, he has no unique core of individuality which the state is obliged to respect. The collective whole is all that counts. A maverick who doesn't fit in must be "liquidated" (note the term), just as a tubercular cow is quietly done away with to keep the herd healthy.

It's very logical, if you believe that man is "nothing but." The Communists are cruel and relentless because they start with a false theology. Theology is the most practical thing in the world; good or bad, it is certain to have consequences.

A vague Humanitarianism is no match for the harshly precise faith of the Communists. Christianity is. Its theology says that man is sacred because God is more sacred. His love for us is the No Trespassing sign warning all princes, presidents, parliaments, and policemen, when they have gone so far, to stop.

4

THE BROADCASTER AND
THE RADIO SETS

It all depends on how you look at it, and that depends on where you were born. One religion is as good as another, one set of morals as defensible as the next.

Anyone who wants to be up to the minute will nod agreement as the above pronouncements are spoken. Here are two comments by students which develop the same chain of reasoning:

Does it really matter what we believe in—whether you call it God, Confucius, or whatever have you? Personally I would rather call it faith—faith in something higher than ourselves—something we can turn to in need and be comforted by. Why do missionaries go to the Orient to change these people to Christianity—why do they think that Christianity is the only way—if these people who have another faith really live in that faith, what difference does it make—it is a personal affair—what might give help to one may be of no use to another.

In sociology class we were told that our type of people found that Christianity "fitted into" their kind of life the best. Perhaps Mohammedanism is just as "right." If I had been born within a different culture, I might have followed a different religion.

The social sciences as commonly taught lead to Relativism, the belief that nothing is absolute—"It all depends on how you look at it."

Anthropology is the storehouse of information to back up the gospel of Relativism. In Anthro 1 you learn about the strange customs and beliefs of other cultures.* One tribe goes in for cannibalism; even beef is taboo a few thousand miles away. Head-hunting is approved in one place; infanticide, in another. Society A tenderly cares for its elders; Society B turns them out to freeze. Almost everything is respectable somewhere: cannibalism, suicide, human sacrifice, torture, war, polygamy, polyandry.

Two conflicting conclusions can be drawn from Relativism. One is that anything goes. If some societies practice head-hunting, then there's nothing wrong with it, and you can start whetting the butcher knife now, here in America. And if your English professor displeases you, offer him as a sacrifice on the altar of your favorite god.

However, even the most convinced relativist seldom goes this far. Folkways and moral codes may all be equally arbitrary (the Eskimos think us as queer as we think them), but *some sort of code*, accepted by everybody in a particular society, is essential. If all the strange customs of every culture were imported into America, only chaos could result.

So the practical verdict is: each society has an internal unity and consistency. The habits and beliefs of the people, no matter how outlandish, dovetail together. If you try to introduce foreign folkways the whole pattern will be thrown into con-

---

* I beg pardon of all social scientists for the slapdash use of the words "culture," "society," and "civilization" in this chapter. The English professor in me has sacrificed technical precision for variety of vocabulary. I trust that, for present purposes, my disregard of scholarly distinctions is harmless.

fusion, and its cohesion destroyed. Examples are cited of South Sea Islanders who sank into listlessness because Mother Hubbard dresses were forced upon them by missionaries, and head-hunters who lost their morale when forbidden to practice their favorite sport. The wise thing is to let each culture continue as it is.

It is true that not all anthropologists and sociologists are happy with the extremes of Relativism. Some of them are now in quest of the universals which exist, despite a welter of contradictory customs. Already enough research has been tabulated to reveal that some attitudes are almost world-wide. Professor Murdock of Yale points out that in a sampling of two hundred and fifty societies only five (2 per cent) look with friendly eyes on adultery. And the incest taboo exists in every single one of the thousands of societies which have been classified. Nowhere does public opinion condone the marriage of father and daughter, mother and son, or brother and sister.*

Much important work remains to be done by social scientists looking for norms beneath the bewildering surface of customs and attitudes. In any case, news of this recent trend has scarcely begun to filter much into the average classroom. Relativism is still king and god.

Opposed to Relativism is a belief in *natural law*. Used in this connection, the phrase doesn't mean the law of gravitation or anything else that the scientists have formulated from their observations. The scientists are concerned with what actually

* In a few societies—a very few—the royal family has been exempt from this taboo. The Egyptian Pharaohs are the best known example. These facts are taken from the pamphlet "Sexual Behavior: How Shall We Define and Motivate What is Acceptable?" (papers and notes from a panel discussion at the 37th annual meeting of the American Social Hygiene Association, Feb. 1, 1950, reprinted from *Journal of Social Hygiene*, Vol. 36, pp. 130–161, Apr., 1950).

happens. The philosophers, who talk of natural law, are thinking of what *ought* to happen. If you drop a stone it falls. If
you find a man who has been beaten up by robbers you *ought*
to apply first aid and help him home. But you may decide to
drive on to the dance and forget him.

This idea of natural law seems to be contradicted by cannibalism, infanticide, and all the rest. But several things need
to be considered. One is that some of the outlandish customs
reported by explorers do not represent a complete difference
in morality, but a response to peculiar conditions. The Eskimos
are a kind-hearted people; they turn the old folks out to freeze
simply because the whole tribe would starve if they tried to
drag the aged parents along in the hunt for food. Or take the
case of a Pacific tribe where the oldsters are compelled to
climb a tall tree and are then shaken down to their death.
This is done out of kindness. The natives believe that upon
reaching the other world you will remain forever at the age
you have attained when death overtakes you. To delay the
death of aging parents would doom them to stumbling through
the afterlife on crutches.

In neither of these examples is a totally different morality
involved. Then there is another factor: poverty of imagination.
In some primitive tribes the word for "human race" is also
the name of the tribe. The outsiders, those strange beings that
lurk on the fringes, are not exactly human, and one does not
owe them the same obligations. But why concentrate on examples from other countries? The American soldier, maintain-
ing a double standard in his relations with "white men" and
"Gooks," is doing exactly the same thing.

And here's something else. The more bizarre examples of
strange customs usually come from remote and primitive societies. The higher the civilization, the more its morality ap-

proaches that of other great civilizations. For example, the Golden Rule is found in one form or another in many places. Confucius expressed it negatively—Don't do anything to other people that you wouldn't want them to do to you.

As a culture evolves from its primitive beginnings, four basic changes are likely to occur in its understanding of morality.* (1) It learns to take *intention* into account; accidental homicide is no longer punished like first-degree murder. (2) It learns to distinguish between the individual and his family, and the idea of group punishment becomes repugnant. (3) It discovers that custom isn't a guarantee that something is right and begins to perceive a "law above the law." (4) The obligations of morality expand, no longer embracing only the tribe, and now there is an awareness that the same obligations apply to dealings with outsiders. (This fourth advance is the hardest; in actual practice, it has nowhere achieved complete acceptance.)

The converging agreement is seen most clearly of all when we take the recognized giants in philosophy and religion— Plato, Aristotle, Buddha, Confucius, Moses, Jesus, Mohammed. Their teachings overlap, driving us to believe that they all respond, with greater or less precision, to some absolute *ought* of human nature.†

Does it have to be "either-or"? Perhaps the truth in this instance is "both-and." It may be that Relativism and "natural law" don't really contradict each other, but are parts of a larger and complex reality.

The two concepts can be fitted together this way. Imagine that God is a radio broadcaster, and that a small radio set is

* For an illuminating discussion of the changes, see A. Campbell Garnett, *The Moral Nature of Man*.

† A good anthology of moral teachings to illustrate this point is found in the Appendix to C. S. Lewis, *The Abolition of Man*.

built into each person. Messages of advice and guidance are
constantly sent over the air waves; but some radio sets are
better than others, and some people listen more attentively
and catch more quickly what comes from the loud-speaker.
The great philosophers and religious leaders are born with
good radio sets and a passionate desire to grasp every word of
the broadcasts.

Sometimes it happens that no one in a particular culture
understands much of what is coming in over the ether. In that
case, distorted and positively evil customs may spring up, in
the mistaken belief that the radio broadcaster has authorized
them. But the higher the civilization, the more likelihood that
the messages are received and understood with tolerable com-
pleteness. (Indeed, this is one main reason that the higher civilizations are higher!)

This parable would explain the extreme variations in custom,
as well as the tendency toward greater agreement as the cave-
man and jungle stages are left behind.

But one or two additional complications should be mentioned. Perhaps the broadcaster leaves his station occasionally,
wraps himself in a cloak of invisibility, and mingles unseen
with people here and there. He may have done this with some
of the towering names we have mentioned; he may have
whispered directly into their ears, so that no static blurred his
message. He seems to have done it especially with the Hebrew
prophets of the Old Testament; they write like men who have
listened to the direct words of the broadcaster.

Or the broadcaster could go one step further. He might lay
aside his cloak of invisibility and show himself face to face.
According to Christianity, this happened once: when Christ
was born. So the teachings of Christ represent, in plain and
unmistakable words, the messages constantly sent over the air

waves by the broadcaster. (Christ's teachings represent this, and more. There is the sharpened emphasis on love, as the ultimate basis of conduct.)

If this parable of the invisible broadcaster corresponds to the truth, very few cultures are completely off the track. The most primitive ones, with scattered exceptions, represent an attempt to catch and practice the instructions received over the air. Any missionary or other person who believes he has received a better and more complete message needs to tread with loving care, combating only what is obviously perverted, and seeking substitutes for established but dubious practices. (Hunting the wild boar or even a good rough game of football can satisfy many of the same longings as head-hunting.)

The great majority of modern missionaries realize all this and act accordingly. They also know that every culture has much to teach us. The tranquillity of the Hindu yogi and the exquisite Confucianist sense of human relationships are imports that jittery and abrupt America can profitably use.

Our parable can be employed in one further way: it provides a vantage point for examining the world's religions (as distinct from moral codes, though actually the two are usually so closely meshed together that a divorce is impossible).

When you first study comparative religion, you are impressed by the differences. Perhaps Judaism, Christianity, and Islam could all be grouped together. They share a common belief in a God who is creator of the universe, not to be confused with the universe which he has created. Christianity and Judaism have especially close ties. They both possess the Old Testament as sacred writings, and Christianity is well-nigh meaningless unless the religious history of the Hebrews is constantly borne in mind.

At the opposite pole is Confucianism, reluctant to speculate about the gods, but strongly insistent on a natural law of human conduct. Confucianism looks like humanism to western eyes, but probably not to the Chinese. To them the ritual and balance of personal relationships partake of a religious quality.

Hinduism is a vast sea with many Gulf Streams running through it. At its highest level it can produce a Gandhi. Buddhism is a reformed and puritanized Hinduism, emphasizing certain virtues and psychological techniques that bring liberation from the world of desires and passions. Early Buddhism (though not some of its later developments) was noncommittal about the gods.

All these are religions with profound insights, capable of nurturing saints and undergirding whole civilizations. But what do they have in common?

In all of them, there is a reaching-out or reaching-up or reaching-within, in order to find the invisible broadcaster. The Something or Somebody thus sought goes by many different names: a cosmic "pattern of things"; Nirvana; the divine spark within; or the God who created heaven and earth.

However, the only way the broadcaster can be known with complete certainty is for him to leave the radio station, put aside his cloak of invisibility, and show himself. We have seen that Christians believe this happened in the person of Christ. God is the broadcaster, and Christ is God; Christ is God, incarnate in human flesh and blood. God the broadcaster plunged down into the human race, and by being born as a baby and growing up as a man he made contact with the flesh and blood of all mankind.*

It sounds arrogant. Great as Buddha and Confucius were,

* To state all this with theological precision, the doctrine of the Trinity must be taken into account. It is dealt with in Chapter 14.

Christ is in a class apart—a class of one. An outraged student wrote:

Christianity is bloated with its own importance. It believes that it alone has found God—why, I don't know!—and attempts to *convert* peoples of other faiths to the "true faith." After all, Christians, as well as other people, are mortal. What makes them think that they alone are right, that they alone have found the answer? Is there ever really any one true answer about God? People must find him for themselves, and no man should set himself up as being so all-fired important that he can dictate to others how they should find God.

But suppose it is true. Suppose Christ is actually God as well as man. The word "arrogant" is no answer; the question is: Did this thing really happen? The evidence that it did must be saved for later chapters, but it is worth pointing out now that a great deal of reality is equally arrogant. It seems unfair that a doctor supplied with penicillin can cure diseases that would baffle a doctor with nothing but sulfa drugs. But the only real arrogance would be if the doctor who had penicillin refused to share it with the other physician.

This brings up the question that is usually phrased: What about the Buddhists? Are they, and other non-Christians, going to hell because they have never heard of Christianity or are unwilling to accept it? "If a person is a law-abiding citizen who is kind to his fellow men, why should he be condemned to hell because he doesn't believe in Christ?" is how one girl expressed it.

Some theologians have grimly replied that salvation is through Christ, and Christ alone, and that people who have no dealings with Christ are obviously beyond the possibility of salvation. If a man has a bad virus infection and refuses penicillin (or if his physician doesn't have any available) the man dies.

But this belief does not represent the norm of Christian thinking. It puts too many limits both on God's power and on his love. Most Christians believe that Christ can come to men and women who have never heard his name, or who—for psychological reasons beyond their own control—think they have rejected him.

Christ can do this precisely because he is not simply a man who lived almost two thousand years ago in Palestine, and whose teachings are recorded in a book. As the Second Person of the Trinity, he is eternal and can go everywhere, even into minds and hearts that do not know his name. Where he is not permitted to work openly, he works secretly. Whoever responds to love—by whatever name it is called—is responding to Christ. And Christ, by name or nameless, is the penicillin of salvation.

So the destiny of the Buddhists can be safely left in the hands of Christ, who is not less solicitous of their welfare than we are. But this does not remove our obligation to make penicillin freely and publicly available. To offer it, and offer it by name, is an act not of arrogance but of love.

5

WISHES AND FULFILLMENTS

If most religions are man's attempt to locate the cosmic broadcaster, the question remains, Is there any broadcaster to be located? The favorite attack on religion is to say that God didn't create man; instead, man created God—in his own image. Religion is a childish thing—a crutch for the bewildered and the feeble, but not needed by a strong man. It may have been a useful illusion in the infancy of the race, and it is natural in a young child, but it ought to be put away with other childish things. Here is the way three students sum it up:

Religion, to me, is a pleasant repetition from childhood. I like the sameness of the ceremony, the choir droning, the preacher droning, the drone of the crowd as it enters and leaves, the familiar tinkle of the coins dropping in the collection box, the feeling of participation I achieve when I put my small hand and small contribution with the others. Religion to me is a series of sounds and participation patterns which are reminiscent of my childhood.

I would like to believe that there is a heaven to go to when I die. I would also like to believe that there is an all-powerful Being that rules the universe. This seems to be the easy way out.

35

In otner words, I feel it's easier on yourself to believe that everything will be roses when you die.

I suppose that some day, when I am older and my mind is too
tired to ask "Why?" and when I am weak enough to submit, I
shall accept Christianity in the weakness of old age as I did in the
innocence of childhood.

How did religion start? The explanation that you hear most
often runs something like this: The shaggy cave man looked
with wonder and terror at the vast wilderness about him, and
invented gods and spirits both to explain what he could not
understand, and to protect himself from his fears.* At a later
stage he sometimes combined the assorted divinities into one
all-embracing God, who was a composite of the earlier gods.

Now this theory may or may not be true. There is no
earthly way of finding out. The cave man has long been
extinct, and we cannot interview him about his faith. Primitive
societies that still exist are no safe guide; their religion may
have evolved past all recognition from the cave-man days.

But assume that the common theory is on the right track. It
still proves nothing either way about the truth of religion.
The cave man's confused gropings toward God probably involved a great deal of fear or superstition; but at least they
were gropings. There is nothing odd in the idea that God
might seize on the most primitive impulses and guide them in
the direction he wanted them to develop. If he found the cave
man worshiping a multitude of spirits, he could whisper, "One
is better than many." And after the one had absorbed the

* The theory that man's earliest religion was polytheism—many gods
—is the one that crops up most often in casual discussions. Its credentials are shaky. Some authorities suspect that polytheism was preceded
by pantheism—the universe as God. No one can be certain; but, whatever the *ultimate* origins, the progression from polytheism to mono-
theism—one God—can be traced in a number of religions.

many he would set himself to the task of giving the cave man a clearer and clearer idea of this one deity, and how men ought to respond to it.

Something of the sort happened in the history of the Hebrews. At first, they apparently regarded Yahweh as a tribal god; but other tribes had other gods. Only gradually did the other divinities fade away, leaving Yahweh as the only God there is—the God of all mankind.

But this is a futile and useless thing to speculate about. No matter what the origin of religion may be, it's the finished product that counts, not the crude beginnings. Modern astronomy grew out of astrology, but you would not ask your professor of astronomy to read your horoscope. Chemistry grew out of the alchemist's quest for a way to turn base metals into gold, but does that make chemistry any less a science? There is a time when every fetus passes through a fishlike stage, but you cannot understand your fraternity brothers by studying ichthyology.

Most often, however, the wish-fulfillment theory is presented in terms of the "Father complex." * The name of Freud is especially associated with this, but a number of other psychologists concur.

According to this way of explaining God, the father of early childhood seems more majestic and powerful and protective than he actually is. When you reach maturity and see Dad objectively—getting bald, and asking nothing better of life than a chance to read the evening paper in peace—you are disillusioned. An aching void is left in your heart. You are exposed to all the coldness and terror of a hostile universe.

---

* My discussion here has been partly shaped by John Pitts's excellent book, *Religion and the New Paganism* (Independent Press, London, 1950).

You still want a protective father. So you turn to an imaginary one in heaven, who is created in the image of your childhood father.

God therefore belongs in the same class as the imaginary playmates that lonely children sometimes invent for themselves. People cling to the illusion because they lack the courage to face the universe with their own puny strength.

Note first of all that this theory is firmly bedded on the psychoanalyst's couch. Freud seldom had reason to examine the psyche of anyone who was getting along all right. His patients were mixed up in every possible way, including their religion. To some of them, God may well have been a substitute for the father of childhood. But this does not prove that God is a substitute father in the case of reasonably normal people.

In the second place, this kind of explanation can be used to explain everything away. A young man may become a Communist because he hates his rich father. A Don Juan may act that way because sexual escapades are a means of overcoming an inferiority complex. But if some people embrace the cause of the masses or indulge in amorous exploits for reasons that have no connection with love of the masses or just plain lust, that still doesn't mean that Communism and lust are mere shadowy projections of the ego. Sometimes men turn to real things for the wrong reasons.

The truth is that people keep busy explaining God away because there is no place for him in their private picture of the universe. If you are convinced that the only kind of reality is the sort you can bang your fist against, then God does not, *cannot* exist. But to settle the argument in such summary fashion is to beg the question; it is shoddy science and infantile philosophy. The first thing to be decided is whether reality is all of the bang-your-fist kind.

The best way to deal with the question is to study the men and women who have met another kind of reality. Take the Gandhis and the Schweitzers. They are the Shakespeares and Beethovens of religion. It is difficult to believe that a man who, singlehanded, challenged the might of the British Empire, or one who gave up three or four brilliant careers in Europe to serve the Congo natives, is hiding away from the stark realities of existence. Such men are magnificently alive, and ready to brave all the terrors of the universe. If they are victims of a childish illusion, then the rest of us are still in the illusions of prenatal life.

Now back for a moment to the overrated father of babyhood and the invisible Father in heaven. If you grant that invisible kinds of reality (such as God) may exist, then Freud's theory can be plausibly set on its head. The Father in heaven is the really solid one. The earthly father is a shadow or symbol of him. The small baby, who is taken for walks by his father, protected from barking dogs, and treated with tender affection, falls into an innocent kind of idolatry. The father by his crib seems God enough for him. But when he grows up he discovers that his father is another man like himself. At this point he quite reasonably goes looking for the real and eternal Father—and finds him.

The "Father-complex" theory is the most specific type of explaining away, and, as we have seen, it really begs the question. But sometimes the idea of religion as "wish fulfillment" is put in more general terms: Faith is simply a kind of cotton padding, to keep you from getting bruised as you jounce over the rough road of life. In particular, belief in a heavenly afterlife is a symptom of "failure of nerve." You can't take it when the going is rough, and so you dream up pie in the sky when you die.

Anyone who wanted to could devise a religion that would actually meet the specifications for wish fulfillment. Suppose a committee interviewed a cross-section of the population, and questioned them about their longings. On the basis of the questionnaire it could construct a faith that would give the customers exactly what they want. I imagine that it would include a rather senile Father in heaven (who knows when to look the other way), and that everybody would automatically be destined for an afterlife combining the best features of a country club and an expensive resort hotel.

But Christianity isn't like that. Once you really begin to look it in the face, you find it a fabric of terrors as well as delights. It has a Father in heaven, but he is not in his dotage. He knows what is going on. He makes tough demands on people—love, as God demands it, takes all one's strength. He offers a heaven, it is true, but the heaven does not resemble a country club. It is a place or state of being where the individual's precious ego becomes translucent in God's radiance, and is no longer important. To the average person, this kind of heaven is a second edition of hell; it is no comfort to the pitiful misfits who need cotton padding. And then there is hell—alienation from God, bleak, lonely, the ultimate idiocy, and a live possibility for everyone.

It would take a committee of madmen to create such a religion in the hope of giving the customers what they want. Christianity is no bed of roses—there are thorns aplenty. We all like *some* things in it, but only the greatest saints like everything in it. It was not invented by consulting a Gallup poll.

And this is the real answer to people who are busy trying to explain Christianity away. One can use Christianity (like art, Communism, love, or anything else) as cotton padding to keep from getting bruised by life; but this is possible only by closing your eyes to the real implications of Christianity. Real Christianity—and that's all we need bother with—is tough and tender, alluring and frightening, comforting and impossibly difficult.

6

SCIENCE AND SCIENTISM

In our modern world, it is very difficult to believe some of the teachings of the church and Christianity as a whole. With all our modern inventions and our scientific discoveries the church in some respects has become almost outmoded.

Of all the reasons that can be offered as to why one should doubt Christianity, probably the one on which I lean most heavily is the one offered by modern science.

These two comments by students lead us to the most important campus god of all: Scientism.

The name sounds almost like "science"; but the two do not have much in common. Science is a useful servant. Scientism is a deity. The real scientists rarely practice the cult of Scientism. The faithful worshipers are the bystanders and hangers-on of science: people who know just enough about what science can do to be sure that it can do everything.

What science *can* do is impressive enough. It is a definite method of obtaining definite information. The procedure used in the more impersonal and exact sciences—such as physics and chemistry—can be simply outlined:

(1) *Observation.* You observe, and observe systematically.

Usually this involves a prepared experiment in the laboratory, but not always. (You can't put the stars in a lab.) The more data you collect, the better. And if you can organize the data in terms of measurements and numbers, better still. Throughout the period of observation you need to avoid emotional involvement with the outcome. Your frame of mind should be objective; you are like an uncommitted delegate to a political convention, willing to listen to the speeches in praise of all the candidates, but determined to suspend your judgment until the evidence convinces you that one particular man is worthy of your vote.

(2) *Hypothesis*. Having carried on your observations for a sufficient period of time, you try to think of a possible explanation for what you have observed. Call this a shrewd guess or "hypothesis." It may come in a sudden flash of insight or intuition.* But the hunch in itself is not enough. It must be tested.

(3) *Verification*. You devise a suitable experiment to test your hypothesis, and decide in advance what the outcome should be *if* it is correct. Perhaps the experiment turns out differently. Then you abandon the hypothesis, and seek a new one. But if the experiment seems to confirm it, and if other scientists, carrying out a variety of experiments, always get results that tally with it, the hypothesis is promoted to the status of a *theory*. This still does not mean it is certain. Scientists do not talk about certainties. The most venerable theory is subject to change without notice, if newer discoveries un-

---

* Contrary to popular impression, the really great scientist has much in common with the poet, artist, and mystic. Albert Einstein says: "The most beautiful and most profound emotion we can experience is the sensation of the mystical. It is the sower of all true science." (Lincoln Barnett, *The Universe and Dr. Einstein*, William Sloane Associates, New York, 1948, p. 105. Quoted by permission of the publishers.)

dermine its foundations; but a theory represents some such judgment as "All available evidence up to now points this way."

Science is really systematized common sense. We can imagine the cave man first noticing that saber-toothed tigers were fond of rabbits (observation), then dimly wondering whether rabbits might not be good food (hypothesis), and finally eating a rabbit with no ill effects (verification of hypothesis, and promotion of it to the rank of theory).

But it is only in the past five hundred years that the full possibilities of the scientific method have been realized. The increases in knowledge have been so sensational that little comment is needed. In the thirteenth century, one scholar might master all the known facts about the universe. Today the attempt would be utterly impossible: nobody lives long enough. The result has been specialization. The physicist, if he is going to learn everything possible about physics, finds little time for botany or sociology. Charles Darwin regretfully abandoned his interest in music and poetry, in order to concentrate on biology.

Science is a definite way of getting at facts. It is also useful. Its popular prestige probably rests mainly on this. Miracle drugs, plastics, radio, television, atomic energy, increased productivity of farms—the practical achievements of science could be extended into a list the length of this book.

In still a third way, science merits the prestige that is accorded it. Scientific research calls forth and develops certain traits of character. The really great scientist has to be humble. He is not out to bolster his ego but to discover facts. In order to discover them, he needs an open mind, a willingness to follow the evidence wherever it may lead him. Any trace of dishonesty in his work—any effort to doctor the facts to make them fit a preconceived theory—is fatal. Indeed, the qualities of character essential to solid work in the sciences closely parallel the lists of virtues often drawn up by philosophers and religious teachers.

Science is a school for character, it is immensely useful, and it has been sensationally successful in solving mysteries that have baffled mankind for many millennia. Then isn't it a complete way of life?

The apostles of Scientism say that it is. But they can say this only because they forget to ask one further question: What can't science do?

For example, can it prove or disprove the existence of ghosts? This question is amusingly treated by Anthony Standen, himself a scientist:

In the supremely confident period, toward the end of the last century, when it was supposed that there was a conflict between Science and Religion, and Science was rapidly winning, it was the mark of an educated man to say "Science has proved that there are no such things as ghosts, they are merely the superstitions of the unenlightened." Education is always behind the times, and much the same attitude is prevalent today; you can still hear people say, "Surely, science has proved that there are no ghosts." And yet, is that so? Suppose, just suppose for the sake of argument, that ghosts can occasionally appear when the psychological conditions are just right, and suppose, what might quite well be true, that one necessary condition for the appearance of a ghost is the *absence* of a scientist: well then, "Science" (that is to say, scientists) would go on investigating ghost after ghost, and would "disprove" every one of them, and yet ghosts would continue to appear whenever the scientists were not looking.*

Ghosts are not an important issue with most of us. Neither

* Anthony Standen, *Science Is a Sacred Cow* (E. P. Dutton & Company, New York, 1950), pp. 32–33. Quoted by permission of the publishers.

are angels and demons (about which science is also incapable
of rendering a verdict). But we come closer home when we
have a look at several other questions that science cannot
answer.

For example, what can science say about beauty? Everyone
responds to something he calls beauty, whether he finds it in
a mountain landscape or a lovely face. Was Plato right when
he contended that "Beauty" exists in an invisible but absolute
state, as an eternal "idea," and that the breath-taking range of
mountains or the exquisite face is nothing but a passing and
imperfect reflection of Absolute Beauty? Science has no tools
for reaching a decision. It is a question for philosophers to
handle.

Or take love. Its intimate connection with sex is not a discovery of science. The Greek dramatists and the writers of
the Old Testament knew the facts of life. But can romantic
love be explained solely in terms of sex? One must speak
plainly here. Talk with any man who has paid a casual visit
to a prostitute, and who subsequently has fallen in love with a
girl and married her. He will say that the quality of the second
relationship is so different that the word "love" can't be applied to both. And yet, the physiology of the two experiences
is the same. The thing that makes all the difference—love—
is precisely what cannot be studied by scientific methods. The
best way to understand love is to fall in love; next best is to
read love poetry or great novels and plays dealing with love.

If science is helpless to differentiate between love and lust,
it is still less capable of answering the most important question of all: Does God exist? The distant stars cannot be carted
into the laboratory for close-range study; but at least they
can be seen through a telescope and analyzed by means of the

spectroscope. God, being invisible and nonmaterial, cannot be captured by the instruments of science. Many lines of philosophic reasoning converge on him; but philosophy is philosophy, and science is science. Personal experience also confirms his existence; but, though science may study the blood pressure and pulse of the mystic, it has no way of saying whether his experience corresponds to anything real.

All this can be clarified by asking whether you believe that Reality has one story or two. By Reality, I mean everything there is, visible or invisible. If you believe that Reality is a house with only one story, you have a philosophy—*Naturalism.* There are many subvarieties of Naturalism, but most of them agree that everything is ultimately material in origin. Thought is simply an activity of the brain; love is a sentimental by-product of the glands; God (by definition a "spirit") is automatically ruled out of court—he *can't* be real.

Now the important thing to remember is that Naturalism is a *philosophy.* Science cannot say whether it is a true philosophy. Science has found no way of determining whether Reality has a second story.

Suppose that the second story is actually there. Great areas of human experience now begin to make sense, because we are able to take into account our adventures on both floors of the house. God is upstairs, waiting for us, and indeed he has a habit of making unscheduled forays down to the first floor, though not in a systematic way that lends itself to scientific verification. The sense of beauty, the fact of love—perhaps they have their ultimate origin upstairs, and what we experience on the first floor is a reflection or embodiment of the everlasting things of the second floor.

The only way to decide the question is to turn philosopher

and ask yourself: Do all the things I have so far experienced make better sense if I assume one story, or two stories, to the house?

If you decide that the second story is real you are not in the least denying the painstaking inventory that the scientists have conducted on the first floor. But if you deny the second story you have to reject most of the experiences that are most overwhelmingly real in your own life. It would be a strange thing to believe in atoms, which are too small to be perceived directly, and not to believe in beauty, love, the conscience, and the mind, all of which are experienced constantly by anyone who does not deliberately close his eyes, ears, and heart.

The great advantage of believing in the second story is that you don't have to explain away most of the things that make you human. You can throw "nothing but" out of your vocabulary. Henceforth, love can be plain love, God can be God. Neither is a mask for something else.

It is clear, then, that the most obvious defect of Scientism (faith in science as a complete way of life) is this: science has no methods for answering the really urgent questions. But there is another thing that science is unable to accomplish. It cannot tell you what you *ought* to do.

Science is concerned with *is*, not *ought*. The problem posed by nuclear fission is an example used so often that it has become trite; but it will serve again. No laboratory experiment can advise you what *ought* to be done with the atom. We can seize upon it to broil whole cities of people, or we can use it to provide additional sources of peacetime power. The physicists who began stumping the country shortly after Hiroshima, urging the second alternative, spoke as men and moralists, not as specialized scientists.

People often grant all this, but then add, "Can't the social sciences provide the necessary guidance, and teach us how to use the discoveries of science properly?"

One should not make a dogmatic answer here. Sociology, psychology, and anthropology are still in their infancy, compared to astronomy and physics. But, so far, the chances of bridging the chasm between *is* and *ought* don't look too good.

It is true, as we saw in Chapter 4, that the social scientists have catalogued certain attitudes which are universal or very nearly so: the incest taboo and the disapproval of adultery are examples. Very likely these world-wide norms do indeed represent the lowest common denominator of "natural law"— the message of the invisible broadcaster.

But they don't go far enough to be of much real help. Every society agrees that some sort of family organization is necessary; but what we need to know is whether it is best to have four wives or one, and whether it is all right to turn in an unsatisfactory wife for a new model.

Even if the public opinion poll is confined to our own culture, the replies are confusing. Ask ten of your classmates whether mercy killing should be legalized, and see how much agreement you will find.

But suppose you abandon the quest of *ought* and concentrate on *is*. You decide that you are going to achieve happiness by being the model of perfect social adjustment—you will behave precisely as most Americans of your age and social class behave. That will be your morality.

Such surveys as the Kinsey report will give you the facts. Dr. Kinsey sent his researchers forth, not to discover how men think they *ought* to conduct their sexual life, but the way they *actually* conduct it. Many intriguing facts were accumulated. Some men go to prostitutes, and some don't; some seduce their girl friends, and some don't; some are faithful to their wives, and some are not. And there are interesting differences between various social levels.

Can the Kinsey report be your guide to personal happiness and fulfillment? If you want to "do what the Joneses do," it will provide you with the data you need about one important aspect of life. But suppose the Joneses are stupid and short-sighted? They often seem to be.

At this point, other social scientists will provide you with statistics on happiness. Certain types of conduct seem to lead most often to happiness. But even this does not answer the question, because it all depends on what you mean by happiness. The word has quite different meanings to: (1) a Don Juan, (2) an explorer, (3) a concert pianist, (4) a monk or nun. There is no way that the social sciences can tell you whether it is better to go on the concert stage or retire into a cloister. And that kind of decision has to be made before you can begin aiming at happiness.

The bridge between *is* and *ought* still looks too frail to support a 170-pound man. Despite this, the social scientists sometimes go on a crusade, and become passionately concerned with "values." The fact is to their credit as men, but the confusion begins when they try to invoke the authority of their particular sciences. Most of the crusading physicists after Hiroshima were clear-headed enough not to argue that "science has proved we ought to put the atom under international control." They simply said common sense had proved it. But the social scientist, concerned already with the study of society, is more likely to get his facts and his feelings mixed up.

At the present moment, a great many professors of sociology and education have descended from the ivory tower and are trying to indoctrinate people with a devout faith in democracy. They quote all sorts of facts and statistics to prove that democracy is the best form of government. And they collaborate with the psychologists to devise methods for filling the oncoming generation with democratic ideals.

"Science has taken a stand," we frequently read in the newspapers when some sociologist or psychologist issues a ringing affirmation of democracy, or inveighs against racial discrimination. But the headline should say, "Scientist So-and-so has taken a stand."

Race relations will usefully illustrate this point. Starting with the actual situation in America, we can see it might develop in either of two directions. We could evolve a rigid caste system, with blacks and whites kept apart by law and the sanctions of custom. This would resemble the caste system of India. And it would be perfectly workable as a social structure. A similar stratification has lasted many centuries in India.

Or America can travel in the opposite direction—gradually get rid of legal segregation and social discrimination, until a time comes when the color of a man's skin is as irrelevant as the color of his hair. This also is perfectly practical as a social structure. Brazil has gone far in that direction.

Which goal do you prefer? If you prefer the second, it is not because some scientist has made a discovery, but because you believe in the brotherhood of man and recognize all forms of discrimination as roadblocks against brotherhood. Back of your belief in human brotherhood stands a belief in the fatherhood of God—perhaps not your own belief, but one which has so permeated the western world that no one can entirely escape its consequences.

Once you decide that racial discrimination is bad, the social scientists will give you sturdy and intelligent help in combating it. They can disprove a great many of the old lies: the charge that Negroes are more given to crime than white people living in similar conditions, the groundless belief that Negroes are less intelligent than whites. These myths can be demolished scientifically.

Also, the social scientists can perfect methods of education that will gradually lessen the amount of racial prejudice absorbed by children. And in the adult world they can develop practical techniques for helping the two races work together, *if* the will to cooperate already exists.

But back of all these activities lies the fundamental belief, which can be neither proved nor disproved by science: that all men are brothers and ought to behave accordingly.

There is a third and last thing that science is unable to do: it cannot provide an ultimate center of loyalty. Who can kneel before a spectroscope or say prayers to a cyclotron? The methods of science are and should be cold and impersonal; the universe that it is able to explore is also impersonal, more akin to mathematics than to music, love, or friendship.

If the universe charted by science were all there is, we should have to reconcile ourselves to it: button our coats up tight and make the best of our loneliness. But there is no good reason to believe that it is the total picture of reality. A high percentage of the really great scientists are convinced that it is not; Professor Einstein is only one among many who find their sense of mystery and of the ultimate reality of God growing stronger as the exploration of the tangible universe is pushed farther and farther.

For scientist and nonscientist alike, there is a built-in human need, as basic and agonizing as the hunger for food and drink. This is the hunger for Someone who can claim absolute love and absolute loyalty, who can lift our eyes and thoughts above the merely human, who can bring alive the hidden "I," provide an answer to the "ought."

By now the distinction between science and Scientism should be clear. Science is concerned with what can be learned by the scientific method, which is technique for exploring the first story of reality. Scientism is a faith, *not founded on science*, that the first story is the only story, and that the absence of certain pieces of furniture from the first floor is proof that such furniture cannot exist.

Scientism is a deadly enemy of science, because it demands too much. We all recall what has happened to biblical literalists who turned to the Bible to find the shape of the earth, its age, and its relation to the sun. They were heaped mountainhigh with well earned ridicule, and the really valid parts of their faith were crushed by the avalanche of laughter. The apostles of Scientism are subjecting science to the same danger. If you expect the impossible from science—if you demand the answers that can come only from art, philosophy, and religion —you are preparing people for wholesale disillusionment. A time will come when many of the tremendous achievements of science will be laughed out of court, because its camp followers demand the impossible.

7

SCIENCE AND THE
THREE-LAYER CAKE

THERE IS NO CONFLICT BETWEEN SCIENCE AND CHRISTIAN-
ity, but people often think there is. The notion arises because
the wrong questions are directed either to science or to Christianity. If the right questions are asked, there is no necessity
for choosing one and rejecting the other.

"I think the teachings of Christ in regard to human relations
are necessary if we are to live with one another peacefully,"
a student stated. "But—I consider a belief in God, still more a
belief in Christ as a son of God, as rather silly." The reason?
"Perhaps I've had too much science in my education, and
can't accept anything without concrete proof."

We are back again to Scientism, and its attempt to take one
road to knowledge and say it is the only one. Scientism directs
the wrong questions to science, and confidently expects an
answer.

Here are two additional comments, typical of many:

When I was younger, my parents sent me to Sunday school
. . . Then, in our science courses, the teachers would tell us how

54

the world came to be. *That* didn't coincide with Genesis. I was puzzled.

The theory of evolution seems so very logical to me and the creation of the earth by God in seven days seems so impossible. It really is difficult to understand. Yet many of the scientists who believe in the theory of evolution are good Christians.

What is said in these quotations is not as interesting as what is implied. The unspoken assumptions are: (1) The Bible ought to give a detailed, timetable description of how the universe and its forms of life came into being. (2) Science ought to be able to answer the ultimate *why*.

Both hopes are unfounded. The Bible, in its earlier parts, uses the language of myth, symbol, and poetry to express the overwhelming conviction that, if it weren't for God, there would be no universe, no life, no anything. The Bible answers the *why*. Science is concerned with the *what*, not the ultimate *why*. It studies the universe which is already in existence. If it advances theories as to how that universe has evolved, it still has nothing to say about why it came into being and began evolving.

The tension between science and religion (caused to a large extent by asking the wrong questions of both) has a long history. It started as early as the sixteenth century, when the experimental method picked up speed. Discoveries were made that seemed to conflict with medieval scholasticism. The beautiful synthesis of all knowledge—religion, philosophy, and science—which Thomas Aquinas had worked out in the thirteenth century was no longer adequate to accommodate the new knowledge.

The first great conflict was over astronomy. Copernicus, contradicting both the science of the time and the language of the Bible, said that the earth revolves around the sun. To many pious souls it appeared that the entire structure of the Christian faith would tumble down in ruins if the sun weren't kept in its proper place. But Copernicus won out, and only a handful of biblical literalists today insist that the sun circles around the earth. The average Christian, if he thinks about it at all, finds the incredibly vast universe of modern astronomy a more impressive manifestation of God than the smaller and tidier cosmos of Ptolemy.

The most painful quarrel between science and religion came to a head about a century ago with the publication of Darwin's *Origin of Species*. Was the human race created by God in a flash of time, or did it evolve from simpler forms of life over the eons? "Our Biology teachers speak of evolution as a proven fact which must be accepted by everyone," one girl wrote. Then she added, "I find it impossible to reconcile the conception of Christianity and evolution."

The fact to remember is that the Bible is not a treatise which describes the emergence of life from the one-cell creature to the six-foot man. That is the job of science. The Bible *is* concerned with stating in vivid, nonscientific language that God is the ultimate reason for the existence of life, and that he has guided its development with certain definite goals in view. One of the goals is the human race. This contradicts nothing in science; nor does anything in science contradict it. The religious value of Genesis remains intact and is clearer and more powerful than ever, once the mistaken notion that it is a textbook of geology and biology has been abandoned.

The furor over evolution is fading away, and the new "conflict between science and religion" centers around the social sciences. Some of the questions we have already looked at are examples: Is morality a purely relative thing? Is every religion a product of its culture? Is God merely a projection of the ego?

If history repeats itself, as it has a way of doing in these matters, the challenge now hurled at religion by the social sciences will be as old-fashioned a century from now as "Genesis versus evolution" is beginning to be today. This does not mean that either side will achieve total victory. People will simply come to see what each can and cannot do. They will learn to ask the right questions of each. Religion will be enriched from the challenge, and there are signs that the social sciences will eventually be deepened by the insights of religion.

Already faint hints of the future rapprochement are visible. As we have seen, some anthropologists and sociologists, sated with listing the strange customs of strange lands, are trying to discover what norms of human conduct are universal. The psychologists, working for the most part without religious presuppositions, are developing a concept of love remarkably similar to the Christian one; some pioneers are taking the further step of investigating the role of religion in a well integrated life. Meanwhile, the church seminaries are introducing courses in psychology and other social sciences, in an effort to give their graduates the benefit of the practical insights made available by the scientists who study human relationships.

The whole question of science and religion is clarified if you realize that the different sciences have developed in three main surges. First there were the sciences dealing with lifeless *matter* —astronomy, physics, chemistry, etc. Copernicus was born in the fifteenth century, Galileo in the sixteenth. The sciences concerned with life—biology, etc.—gained momentum next, and really came into their own in the nineteenth century with such men as Pasteur and Darwin. Last of all were the sciences that study *human life*—sociology, anthropology, psychology, etc. Their real flowering has been in the twentieth century, and one of their first giants, Freud, died only a few years ago.

The "conflict of science and religion" has followed the advancing frontier of the sciences. The fight over astronomy is obsolete, and God's universe looks more majestic than ever. Evolution is ceasing to be a battle cry, and it has not destroyed the uniqueness of man, and God's creative hand. There's still much tension between the social sciences and Christianity, but cases of friendly association between them are cropping up.

Let's divide the main areas of science into a three-layer cake:

HUMAN LIFE

LIFE

MATTER

There are several interesting things about this stratification. We have noticed that the sciences developed from the bottom up, and controversy with Christianity has followed the same timetable; but there is another thing: the sciences on the bottom layer are the most precise, the easiest to handle by an austerely exact method, and those at the top are the least.

Doubtless this is due in part to the fact that physics and astronomy had an early start. The social sciences are in the Newtonian stage—their Einstein hasn't had time to come along; but there is reason to believe that a thousand years from now the sciences of the bottom layer will still be more exact and "scientific" than those at the top.

Atoms and stars don't argue back with you; they don't develop neuroses or go insane. The unpredictables increase when you approach life, especially its more complex forms. Even so, the physiologist studying the digestive system of the hamster or the zoologist observing the play habits of chipmunks has an easier time than the social scientist who wants to predict whether John will pop the question to Mary and, if so, what chances of success their marriage will have.

People often talk as though the human being were nothing

but a citified ape with trousers on. It is true that man has a great deal in common with the ape: both eat, breathe, breed; both have useful hands. But the differences are more striking than the similarities. It would be interesting to interview a chimpanzee in the zoo. What must he think of these strange beings who wear bright bits of clothing, stand chattering of politics, TV, perhaps even God, and sometimes set up an easel to paint his portrait? He would not be overwhelmed by a sense of kinship: his visitors presume upon his good will if they try to be too chummy.

Now there is a philosophic quarrel which runs all through this. I say "philosophic," though the dispute is sometimes wrongly presented as a scientific one. The question, when you try to see the relationship between the three layers of the cake, is: Should you work entirely from the bottom up?

The devotees of Scientism say you should. Their diagram would look like this:

HUMAN LIFE

↑

LIFE

↑

MATTER

This means that if you could learn everything about matter—push physics, chemistry, etc., to their ultimate frontiers—you would be able to explain, *in terms of lifeless matter*, how life first came into being. Then, by a thorough study of life in general, you would be able to understand all the peculiarities of human life: art, religion, the conscience, the urge that leads to science itself.

This is the "nothing but" theory which we have already mentioned: Life is nothing but matter in a sophisticated condition; man is nothing but a highly developed anthropoid. It is a simple way of looking at things, and has the appeal of all simplifications.

But simplicity and truth are not synonyms. Many real things are unbelievably complicated. Look at the way food is digested or babies come into being. Research into the nucleus of the atom makes it seem more complex all the time, and the scientists still are not sure whether light is waves, particles, or a third something-or-other that no one can imagine.

Reality is often as queer as a surrealist painting. Simplicity cannot be used as proof of anything. Again we are thrown back to the question that we faced in the last chapter: Does Reality have a second story? If it does, and if God lives there (with frequent visits downstairs), the diagram of the layer cake could be modified this way, without denying any of the truths discovered by science:

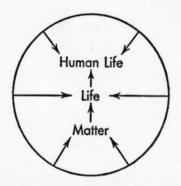

The circle symbolizes God. He first created matter. Then he molded it into things which he endowed with life. Next he guided life so that (among other things) man came into existence. The diagram also suggests that at every moment God is concerned with all three layers of the cake. Man has evolved, but God is not done with him. God is the most likely source of much that seems distinctly human: art, worship, the restless love of change, the sense of anxiety as we project our minds into the future, the passionate love of truth which is the driving power of science.

One diagram tallies as well with science as the other. But the second, like the theory of Reality's second floor, offers a way of understanding every hope, joy, and terror in your life, without trying to pretend that they are really masks for something else.

When the side issues and temporary misunderstandings are stripped away, there can be no conflict between science and Christianity. The goal of both is truth, and all truth is ultimately God's. God, by name or nameless, is the gadfly and the goad; he will give mankind no peace until it explores and embraces all the truth available. The laboratory is a temple, the temple is a laboratory. They need to work together. Slowly, painfully, but steadily, they are learning how to do it.

8

ATMOSPHERIC REASONS FOR NOT BEING A CHRISTIAN

AT ONE TIME, EVERY FOOL KNEW THAT THE SUN WENT around the earth, that witches were a major social problem, and that insane men could be cured by whipping the demons out of their bodies.

Today, every fool still knows a great many things, most of which are not so. They form a "climate of opinion" or atmosphere. This "climate of opinion" is especially thick on the campus.

One thing any fool knows is that Christianity is old stuff, and therefore irrelevant. If you must have a religion, let it be a new one, compounded of Darwin, Marx, Freud, and John Dewey, and adapted to the age of plastics and electronics.

This attitude is a hold-over from the Gospel of Progress, which was always fuzzy and never distinguished clearly between the invention of gadgets (automobiles, airplanes, radios, etc.) and the discovery of truth (such as the nature of God, and how people ought to get along together). It is possible to progress in one way—the Nazis were good gadget inventors— while standing still or retrogressing in other directions.

Around 300 B.C. a Greek named Euclid developed more than three hundred propositions about geometrical relationships in a book that is still the basis of modern geometry texts. No mathematician would think of saying, "Euclid—that's old stuff."

Therefore, the question is not whether Christianity is old, but whether it is true. Its age is neither a guarantee of its truth, nor proof that it can't be true.

Closely related is another thing that every fool knows: Christianity isn't practical. It has been tried for almost two thousand years—and look at the mess the world is in.

This charge has much truth in it. The world is indeed in a mess; but it has always been in one. Human cussedness, springing from the ingrown self-centeredness that theologians call Original Sin, is the main reason, strongly reinforced by ignorance and stupidity.

But the world is in a mess in spite of Christianity, not because of it. If there were a time machine in which we could travel back to pre-Christian Rome our impressions would be summed up in two words: magnificence and brutality. The ancient Romans' architectural and engineering feats rival our own; but they were the backdrop to men fighting each other in the arenas, other men being torn to pieces by wild beasts and unwanted infants callously left to die. The Judaeo-Christian tradition has been the dominant force in shaping western civilization. To it, more than to any other influence, we owe the priceless boon of an uneasy conscience, together with the slow, reluctant growth in social responsibility. The man who hates social security, growls at appropriations for the public schools, and wants to know why the taxpayers should provide free hospital care for the shiftless poor—such a man has reason to hate Christianity, for it has always insisted that he is his brother's keeper.

Compassion, concern for our neighbor, a wider and wider understanding of the word "brother"—these are the social achievements of the Judaeo-Christian tradition. It is a plain fact that outside western civilization these attitudes are much less developed. It is also true that, where they are now beginning to appear, Christianity has usually had a hand. Gandhi was strongly influenced by the New Testament; the missionaries who went to China roused the Chinese conscience from its excessive preoccupation with family obligations; even Communism, with its supposed zeal for the masses, derives its passion for remaking the world from the religious tradition which Marx thought he was rejecting.

Not that Christianity has been able to do everything; war, racial tension, and class struggle are emphatically with us. But the answer to these challenges is more Christianity, not less—and also more Christians who mean business.

Most people who say Christianity has failed haven't the faintest intention of giving it a try. Either they go idealistic in a vague, sweeping way, with much talk about "world cooperation," as though talk could bring it into being overnight; or they frankly prefer to look out for Number One somewhat in the spirit of the following student quotation:

Then there is the old saw about loving thy neighbor as thyself. This gives the modern college student a big laugh. Don't love your neighbor, compete with him—foreclose a mortgage on his house if you can. Of course, a good deed now and then is helpful to your prestige; public opinion will go for that in a big way.

Another bit of atmospheric folklore is: "Intelligent people can no longer believe in God." The odd thing is that the glib repeaters of this adage usually believe in God, although they may prefer to talk of a "Life Force," "Anti-Chance," "a higher power," "something back of everything else," or "an ultimate intelligence that guides history." All these are aliases for the monosyllable, God. The short, blunt word is avoided because of unpleasant emotional associations (remember the fiery-furnace family) or because, in the prevailing climate, it sounds unscientific. Genuine atheism is rare. The great majority of people are really troubled—once they dig beneath the linguistic confusion—not by the question whether God exists but by what he is like, how you get to know him, and what he will do with you after you meet.*

It is easy to believe in some sort of God, and most people do; but it is hard to believe in Christianity. The God that Christianity proclaims is an outrageous noncomformist. He refuses to stand on the sidelines of his universe. He watches what is going on; he intervenes, when you least expect it. He can do things as wild as a science fiction story.

Without putting it into words, many of us wish that God would keep in his place. He seems to lack decorum. He barges in and does the strangest things. As one student protested: "Christianity seems almost crude in the way that it places emphasis on the spectacular. It's almost like a carnival barker at a freak show."

The freaks go by the title of miracles.† It is true that God does not go along with a saltshaker, scattering miracles right

---

* The philosophic arguments for the existence of God, while not watertight, are impressive enough to suggest that reason and logic point more toward God than away from him. The subject entry "God" in the *Catholic Encyclopedia,* available in almost any college library, gives a full discussion of these arguments. Shorter summaries are found in G. B. Caird, *The Truth of the Gospel,* pp. 11–13.

† There is good evidence that miracles still happen today, especially miracles of healing. Several of the books listed under "Miracles and the Supernatural" in Appendix B contain well documented examples. It would take us too far afield to deal here with contemporary miracles, and we shall therefore confine ourselves to miracles recorded in the Bible.

and left. Ordinarily he works in quieter, more predictable ways. The laws of nature that science examines are real laws, so reliable that the rare exceptions can be disregarded for practical purposes. In our world the law of gravitation is not turned on and off like water in the shower bath; it is on all the time, or so close to all the time that you can be reasonably sure, if you jump from a high building, what will happen next.

But God reserves the right to do the unexpected. The fact that he occasionally exercises this right disturbs our love of order and certainty, and we cry out indignantly, "Any fool knows science has proved that miracles can't happen." Actually, science has proved nothing of the kind.

Imagine a visitor from Mars hovering in a helicopter over a large American city. He notices the traffic lights at the intersections. When a red light shows, the cars halt. When the signal changes to green the cars start moving. Being of a scientific frame of mind, the interplanetary observer frames a hypothesis: "Cars move when the light is green and stop when the light is red." Further observation confirms the hypothesis, and it becomes a well established theory.

But once in a while something queer happens. The cars all pull over to the right-hand side of the street, and one or two vehicles charge through, regardless of red lights. A moment later, the other cars resume their normal habits—go on green and stop on red.

The Martian is puzzled. He cannot know that the traffic experts have drawn up a code which provides for emergencies: an ambulance, a police car, or a fire truck has the right to disregard all red lights. Such disregard is not violation of the law of the city; it is in accord with a paragraph of the law designed to meet unusual needs. The theory of the Martian—go on green and stop on red—is perfectly correct, as far as it goes.

The vehicle plunges through red lights because of an emergency or a special occasion: a fire has broken out, or the Governor has suddenly appeared and must be escorted through the city. The miracles recorded in the Bible cluster around the crises and turning points of history, as history appears to God.

The Old Testament, written for the most part long after the happenings it describes, may very well contain a number of imaginative additions to the plain facts. However, the general pattern can be discerned even there. Note especially the uncanny series of "breaks" that aided the Israelites in their escape from Egypt. The fleeing tribes, en route to the Promised Land, went through all the red lights.

The New Testament is much closer to the events which it relates. There may be some legendary embellishments, but relatively few. There simply hadn't been enough time for people to improve upon reality. To see what occurs when the imagination roams freely, one need only read the later "apocryphal gospels," which have never been part of the New Testament. The so-called "Gospel according to Thomas" has a charming story of how Jesus, at the age of five, constructed a dozen sparrows out of clay, clapped his hands, and—behold! they all started flying. This is precisely the brand of miracle that does *not* figure in the familiar four Gospels.

But it is futile to consider the individual miracles attributed to Christ without first looking at the supreme miracle: the Incarnation. Almost everyone believes in some sort of God, and almost everyone admires Jesus as a moral teacher. But a combination of the two—Jesus the teacher as God incarnate—offends our sense of order and decorum. It seems too bizarre to be true; but, bizarre or not, this ultimate miracle is the foundation on which the Christian faith is built. Here is how one student spoke of it:

Only last year I began to question my own religion. I have always found that Jesus was a comforting friend to have around. But last summer, having talked with several friends and my parents, I began to wonder if my beliefs were well founded. I believe now, or think I believe, that Jesus was a brilliant man who knew human psychology. I believe that he did a lot of good, but I'm not sure that what he did was divine.

The trouble with the Incarnation is that it happened like a flash of lightning. True, there had been a little advance thunder. Some of the Old Testament writers had prophesied a "Messiah" who would be God's agent in carrying out his will on earth. But when the moment came, it came suddenly, and most of the people in Palestine still could not believe the thing had happened. Even Christ's disciples didn't fully understand who he was until his resurrection pried their dull eyes open.

Once God had been God, and man had been man. After Christ was born, there was one being who was *both* God and man.

Why did God do this? The human race was in such desperate condition that it needed outside help. Sometimes when grammar-school children get into an impossibly complicated mix-up on the playground, the teacher comes dashing through the door to straighten things out. The Incarnation was, and is, God's rescue operation.

But did it actually happen? Unless you believe that such things just *can't* happen, the evidence is massive and convincing.

The four Gospels (at least three of them written while friends of Christ were still alive) vary in details, but the general picture of Christ which they present is the same. On the one hand he is supreme moral teacher. Even the handful of genuine atheists will usually concede this. The ethical teachings of Christ have an absoluteness and an authority which win assent from almost everyone, regardless of theology and extent of living up to what Christ taught.

That is one side of it. The other side is this: Christ made the most sweeping claims for himself, the kind of claims that only God can properly make. He forgave people's sins. He talked as though everybody except himself was sinful. He said he had been in existence before Abraham was born. He told the high priest that he was the Messiah. He said he was the way, the truth, and the life.

C. S. Lewis has expressed the dilemma well:

On the one side clear, definite moral teaching. On the other, claims, which, if not true, are those of a megalomaniac, compared with whom Hitler was the most sane and humble of men. There is no half-way house and there is no parallel in other religions. If you had gone to Buddha and asked him 'Are you the son of Bramah?' he would have said, 'My son, you are still in the vale of illusion.' If you had gone to Socrates and asked, 'Are you Zeus?' he would have laughed at you. If you had gone to Mohammed and asked, 'Are you Allah?' he would first have rent his clothes and then cut your head off. If you had asked Confucius, 'Are you Heaven?' I think he would have probably replied, 'Remarks which are not in accordance with nature are in bad taste.' The idea of a great moral teacher saying what Christ said is out of the question. In my opinion, the only person who can say that sort of thing is either God or a complete lunatic suffering from that form of delusion which undermines the whole mind of man. . . .

What are we to do about reconciling the two contradictory phenomena? One attempt consists in saying that the Man did not really say these things, but that His followers exaggerated the story, and so the legend grew up that He had said them. This is difficult because His followers were all Jews; that is, they belonged

to that Nation which of all others was most convinced that there
was only one God—that there could not possibly be another. It is
very odd that this horrible invention about a religious leader
should grow up among the one people in the whole earth least
likely to make such a mistake. On the contrary we get the impression that none of His immediate followers or even of the New
Testament writers embraced the doctrine at all easily.*

The fact of the Incarnation is underlined by the Resurrection. In their attempts to describe Christ's appearances after
the Resurrection, the four Gospels differ in minor details, precisely like four honest witnesses in court; but they agree on
the one overwhelming event.

However, the New Testament is not the only evidence for
the Resurrection. The very existence of the church down the
street is evidence; the fact that Christianity did not peter out
with the crucifixion of Christ is evidence. On Good Friday
his followers were a heartbroken, dispirited little band, fearful of the mob, fearful of the police, crushed by disappoint-
ment and failure. Within a few months they were fanning out
into the callous and cruel Roman Empire to preach the tri-
umphant news of the Messiah who had been raised by God
from death, and had thereby blasted, through the mountainside
of evil and death, a highway to God, on which all were free
to travel. Only the Resurrection can account for this about-
face, the most astonishing that history records of any group
of people. The weight of the evidence is so massively on the
side of the Resurrection that if we refuse to believe it happened this can only be because "every fool knows that such
things *can't* happen."

Christ, then, is the ultimate miracle. And it is natural that

* C. S. Lewis, "What Are We to Make of Jesus Christ?" in *Asking
Them Questions: Third Series,* ed. Ronald Selby Wright, Oxford University Press, New York, 1950, pp. 50–51. Quoted by permission of the
publishers.

minor miracles should cluster about him. One of them, associated with his origin, seems to bewilder and trouble many inquirers out of all proportion to its importance. This is the Virgin Birth. It means simply that Christ had no human father. (It must not be confused with the Immaculate Conception, the belief—held by the Roman Catholic Church—that Mary, from the first instant of her conception, was preserved by God from all stain of Original Sin.)

The biblical evidence for the Virgin Birth is confined to Matthew and Luke. There are many Christians who firmly believe in the divinity of Christ, but suspect that the accounts of the Virgin Birth represent a legend that gradually grew up. Actually, in the typical religious discussion, when people think they are arguing about the way Christ was conceived, they are really debating—in the back of their minds—the question of his divinity. *That* is the real stumbling block. A good example of topsy-turvy reasoning is seen in this statement:

I do not believe in the divinity of Christ. It is ridiculous to suppose that a human being could have been born to a human being by any other means than biological means.

The Virgin Birth is insufficient evidence of the divinity of Christ. But if Christ *is* divine, it seems plausible enough that God might have employed some special procedure to bring about the Incarnation. The whole matter is not worth getting upset about. The Incarnation is the primary fact; how God implemented it is secondary.

The remaining miracles are those attributed to Christ during his ministry—a period variously estimated from one to three years. Most of them are curiously sober and matter-of-fact. Any good scenario writer could invent more impressive ones. Nearly all of them seem to have come about because of

Christ's compassion for people, or because of some practical problem that needed to be met: he healed people when he found them sick; he provided extra food when the bystanders were hungry; he walked on water to rejoin his disciples.

The miracles were practical responses to practical situations; but most of them also possess symbolic overtones. As we read about them and imaginatively re-create them, they echo in the mind and evoke a deepened understanding of the nature and power of God. When Christ raised Lazarus from death, he was reaffirming God's sovereignty over life and death; when he changed water into wine at the Cana wedding feast, his deed also symbolized his offer to transmute the water of mere existence into the wine of "eternal life"; the walking on water was a revelation of God's control over his laws of nature. A miracle is a fact, pointing beyond the fact.

One great value of miracles is that they open our eyes. When Christ multiplied the loaves and fishes, no one could doubt that God was directly at work. But when the revolving seasons bring rain and warm weather, and seeds begin sprouting in the soil, God is also at work. We pay little attention to God's habitual activities—familiarity dulls our eyes; but, when we stop to think of it, the seed sprouting in the moist soil is as incredible a work of God as any wonder recorded in the Bible.

Almost invariably the men and women who have gone farthest toward God, and have the deepest insight into his power and love, are the ones to whom the wall between the natural and the miraculous has gradually become paper-thin. The universe itself is more miraculous than a man walking on water; a baby coming into the world is as emphatically the achievement of God as a dead man summoned back into life. Whatever God touches partakes of the miraculous; and he has a way of touching everything.

9

PSYCHOLOGICAL REASONS FOR NOT BEING A CHRISTIAN

THE CAMPUS CLIMATE BRINGS STORMY WEATHER FOR religion; when God is mentioned the moisture condenses, and globules of wisdom—"what every fool knows"—come slanting down like rain. And simultaneously, the conditioned reflexes begin jerking in protest at the dangerous monosyllable.

The reflexes react convulsively at talk of God, because they have been taught to reserve their cheerful coordination for other stimuli: objectivity, self-reliance, and freedom, to name three of the most important.

Objectivity is a virtue you probably heard little about until you reached the campus. It is seldom in evidence around the cracker barrel or the bridge table back home, where people dissect politicians, or the neighbors; but at college you quickly discover that objectivity is the prime academic virtue; if your term papers don't have it, that A grade goes glimmering.

Objectivity requires an open mind. Don't go off the deep end; keep your shirt on; and, above all, don't commit yourself until all the facts are in. During four years this attitude is pounded into you:

In college we are trained more or less to be analytical and almost scientific in our thinking and reasoning. We are taught to be doubters. We are taught to ask "Why?" To accept without proof would be death to the principles of education.

The quotation is a tribute to the sound education received by the student who wrote it. The determination to ask "Why?" of everything is the passkey to the sort of truth you can depend on once you track it down.*

The only trouble with objectivity is that most of life is not lived in the laboratory, library, and classroom. Outside the sheltered walls things have a way of happening, and happening fast. You find yourself in a position where you have to do something—or else play into the hands of people who have no concept of the virtue of objectivity. Suppose by some chance you are on hand when a lynching party begins to form. If you wish, you can practice objectivity, jot down the details in a notebook, and write a scholarly article when the deed is done. But you are not likely to be present at a lynching. Therefore let us take an example closer home. You are invited to join a fraternity or a sorority which has a restrictive clause about membership. Although little is said about it, it is there, and you know it. You can keep silent, and join up. But you know that by doing this you will forfeit your full rights as a human being.

Certainly, when a practical problem comes up and there is

* It is true, of course, that many professors have firm views on a variety of subjects, and some of them expect to see their views dished back to them at exam time. But, rightly or wrongly, they believe they have arrived at their opinions by a rigorously objective examination of the facts—and that anyone who practices equal objectivity will naturally come to the conclusions that they have already reached.

sufficient time, one should accumulate all the facts possible and not make a snap decision. But there isn't time to learn everything about everything. Moments keep arriving when you have to act on the strength of what you already know. Otherwise you will be gray-haired before you choose a profession, and will be leaning on a crutch by the time you decide to marry.

But it isn't just a lack of time. Often there is no way to get all the facts unless you first leave the peanut gallery. Nobody watching a football game from the bleachers can possibly understand that manly sport like a player when half a dozen sturdy adversaries make a pyramid on his prostrate form.

It's that way with Christianity. Like every religion, it can be fully understood only from the inside. Objectivity—this study of facts from the outside—carries you to the edge of the deep water, and strongly suggests that good swimming is available. But to find out what the water is really like, you have to take a deep breath, dive in, and swim for yourself. To make a cult of objectivity is to purchase a life membership in the Association of Bystanders.

But there is another cult—self-reliance—which can paralyze you just as completely as objectivity, though somewhat more subtly.

Every civilization has its favorite type of hero. The Middle Ages vacillated between the knight and the saint; the old-fashioned Chinese esteemed the Confucianist scholar-gentleman. Our national hero is the go-getter, who starts as a bootblack and ends as president of the First National Bank.

Who are the big wheels on your campus? Aren't they students with unswerving ambition and drive? From the first footprint on the campus grass they set themselves to achieve definite goals; and, the less impressive they are as freshmen, the more they are admired in the senior year when the campus paper tells of their election to the national students' Who's Who.

Now it is obvious that pulling at your bootstraps and concentrating on the job at hand can carry you far—to the presidency of the senior class, even to the White House. The confusion begins when people start drawing analogies. The senior class president tells himself, "I've done all this by my own strength and determination; I can do *everything* the same way."

But he can't. The inward "I" cannot be molded by sheer will power. Many people think it can be. They try to achieve perfection of character and a certain quality of life the same way they aim at a seat on the stock exchange—they grit their teeth and work at it hard. And they fail.

Christians also fail. But the Christian has one advantage. He knows he can't do it alone. There is only one expert who can mold the "I" and guide its quiet, steady growth. The progress the Christian achieves may seem slower than that of his grimly determined, self-sufficient neighbor. But the progress he makes is more permanent, because it reflects the basic alterations that God produces in the "I." In the long run, the somewhat relaxed tortoise will outstrip the tense hare.

But why can't we lift ourselves by our bootstraps and win perfection of character? Because there is something wrong with each of us at the center—something that only God can remedy. *Christianity makes no sense if you think you are all right.*

In each of us there is a stubborn self-centeredness. It shows itself most transparently in small children, who make it clear that parents, planets, and stars ought to revolve around them. It is revealed more subtly and dangerously in grown-ups.

(How about your big wheels? Do they ever try to manipulate other students to increase their own prestige?)

We are jealous of God himself. He is our rival. We are rebels. This kind of rebellion is not going to be overcome by graduate school and a Ph.D.; nor will many expensive hours on the psychoanalyst's couch cure it. And yet, we are not happy rebels. Down underneath, we intuitively know that the future holds little for us except tenseness, inward frustration, and ulcers, unless we call in the services of the only expert who is competent to make the necessary adjustments and alterations.

Most of us, when we really think about it, can see that objectivity and self-reliance are vitamins in moderation but viruses when gulped to excess. Freedom, however, seems the cure-all and universal tonic. But freedom, like objectivity and self-reliance, easily becomes the mask for *pride*, which Christian psychology has shrewdly sized up as the most deep-rooted sin and the highest hurdle between man and God.

Writing home to explain why the dean has suspended you from school is a blow to your pride, but only a faint hint of what it means to turn to God and say, "You take over." As a student put it:

I believe the greatest stumbling block lies not in a person's acceptance of a creed but being able to humble himself before God. . . . To let his will be done, not ours.

Putting yourself in God's hands is an act of surrender; his Church is the P.O.W. camp. If anyone tells you this is easy, the right answer is a horselaugh. "Freedom" is a word properly dear to us; nobody likes to walk across no man's land, white flag in hand.

Marriage involves a similar loss of freedom, and some

people shy away from it precisely as they shy away from God. "I don't want to give up my freedom." When you get married you are no longer at liberty to pick up the telephone book in the late afternoon with half a dozen intriguing possibilities in mind. But here is the paradox. Marriage also *brings* freedom—and wider horizons. In place of an unlimited number of superficial or medium-depth discoveries, it offers you the chance to plumb one human relationship to its depth. Added to this is the opportunity to explore the whole new world of parenthood; you can enter the mainstream of life, instead of paddling in the tributaries.

"Freedom" is merely an abstract word until you *use* freedom, and that involves making choices. Suppose your main interest is the theater. You have a choice of two summer theater companies. One is run by a good-natured, rather bumbling director. He pretty much lets each actor direct himself. The other has a much tougher boss—"the old despot" is the gentlest name ever applied to him; but he has so deep and sensitive a feeling for the stage that he can weld his actors into a team, and get a performance from each person, that would have been impossible if they had been left to their own caprices.

Which of these summer theaters offers you the greater freedom? Obviously the second. As a member of it you can become what you have *freely* decided you want to be—a good actor.

Freedom is to be used, not put into the deep freeze. You freely decide what you want to become, then seek the help of the appropriate expert. You have a picture in the back of your mind of the personality and character you are aiming at. Every religion and philosophy posts its picture on the bulletin board; you can look the pictures over and choose the one that most appeals to you.

To take one example, the Gospel of Progress offers, as model, the man who cheerfully and rationally labors hard so that his great-grandchildren may work only three hours a day in the utopia he is building, and spend the rest of their time eating delicious dinners prepared by pushing buttons, or reading history books that tell how dreadful the old days were, and being very bored.

The picture that Christianity posts on the bulletin board is Christ. But a word of warning here. Make sure it is a complete photograph, not a fragment blown up to full size. For a long time now, it has been fashionable to depict Christ as a good but pale young man, whose eyes glow with mingled tenderness and sorrow. It is certain that Christ could be gentle and tender, and that he grieved for the blindness he saw around him. But he could also denounce double-talkers in language that would bring a libel suit today; and when he drove the go-getters out of the temple he didn't depend on sorrowful looks. In the complete photograph there should be not merely tenderness and sorrow, but also towering strength, boldness, playfulness, and flashing humor.

Christianity is "the imitation of Christ." No one succeeds completely; but some progress far. The great saints and many plain men and women, not officially labeled as saints, have gone far enough to give us some clear intimations of what happens. In them we see the same loving obedience toward God, the overflow of love into concern for all their fellows, the same radiance and indomitable strength, the same tenderness, joy and courage, that are supremely revealed in the man who sat for the Christian portrait.

And here is the mystery and the paradox. The person who uses his freedom to give his "I" into the hands of God, there to be remade in the image of Christ, is really only lending it. For God gives it back. One day, when you least expect it, he returns it to you, much improved from the scrubbing and alterations it has received. What began as surrender to a master ends as sonship to a father.

10

HEARTFELT REASONS FOR NOT BEING A CHRISTIAN

Everybody is socially conscious nowadays. Therefore, a charge often leveled against Christianity is that it is too "spiritual," otherworldly, and antisocial; that it is a morbid preoccupation with personal salvation, accompanied by a refusal to look at all the practical things that need to be done in the world of everyday affairs.

The charge is true for some Christians—but a diminishing number; and they have a wrong idea of Christianity. They are like college students who believe that the main object of four years in school is to establish business contacts for future use.

Real Christianity is fiercely materialistic as well as spiritual. It is so materialistic that it believes God actually acquired a flesh-and-blood body. It is convinced that material things can be instruments of the spirit; that marriage, for instance, is not a crude biological and social necessity but a training ground toward knowledge of God. Romantic love can be a stepping-stone toward the Beatific Vision. The materialism of Christianity is also dramatized by the sacraments. The water of baptism is not a mere symbol; it is actually the means for washing away the dirt of the old life and planting the seeds of the new life. The bread and wine of Holy Communion are an extension of the Incarnation: in some mysterious, but overwhelmingly real way, they convey the life of Christ himself to his followers.

Anyone who wants a really spiritual religion can find it in some varieties of Hinduism and Buddhism. But Christianity is as solidly materialistic * as its parent faith, Judaism. God made the material world, and what he made is good.

Christianity is also passionately social, and has been from the beginning. The lone-wolf Christian, reveling in the flight of the alone to the Alone, is never mentioned in the New Testament, and he is an anomaly at any time. The very concept of the Church as the "Body of Christ" emphasizes the social nature of Christianity. Each member of the Church—by which, of course, I mean the universal Church, not any particular denomination—is like the finger or foot or arm of one body, and the head is Christ. Even when a Christian kneels alone in prayer by his bedside, he prays as a part of the universal Body to which he belongs. The Church is not an afterthought or an "extra." A lone-wolf Christian is as self-contradictory as a one-man college.

Nor is the social character of Christianity confined to Church life. If the faith is real, it spills over into everything else. Sunday cannot be walled off from the rest of the week. Slums, juvenile delinquency, class and race tensions, overcrowded schools, problems of capital-labor relations, what to do about soil erosion, the threat of war—these challenges are

---

* By "materialistic" I mean a belief that material things—atoms, stars, human bodies—are basically good and worthy of attention. This kind of materialism has nothing in common with the pursuit of the dollar sign.

felt the more keenly by anyone who really knows God first hand. Contact with God's eternity sharpens the eyes and the conscience for the here and now.

However, it is also true that Christianity is otherworldly. It is as deeply rooted in the other world as in this one; every Christian has a double citizenship. And part of the other world is heaven and hell.*

Many people rebel at the idea of hell, because they are kind-hearted, or because the whole concept is repugnant. "I've always been confused about heaven and hell," one student admitted. "If God is as merciful as the Bible and ministers state, why need there be a hell? No one who is really sane would commit any unforgivable sins."

The belief in heaven—and hell—is based on three main considerations: (1) Christ constantly taught that everyone is going to live forever—in one state or the other. The person who has found Christ reliable in other ways, as in his moral teachings and his understanding of human psychology, is willing to take his affirmation of heaven and hell on faith. It must be on faith in any case, for heaven and hell can no more be proved or disproved by pragmatic means than a baby in the womb can explore the outside world. (2) Anyone who has established a genuine, personal relationship with God comes to know, at least by flashes, a quality of experience that seems to lie outside the boundaries of time and space. "Everlasting life" has already begun for him, and if it is everlasting it will have no end. (3) Man is free to choose God or to turn away from him. But this freedom is shadow play if it lasts only for a life span. Real freedom means the right to defy God after

---

* Some churches also teach a belief in purgatory where certain souls undergo further purification and preparation before entering heaven. Purgatory, if it exists, is not a permanent home for anyone; it is the anteroom of heaven. The two final alternatives are heaven and hell.

the earth is long since sheathed in ice or turned to a flaming globe by an explosion of the sun.

The trouble starts when you try to visualize heaven and hell. Unless you know the difference between poetry and a photograph, it is best not to try too hard. The language of the New Testament is poetic; it hints at what cannot be literally imagined. (Remember the baby in his mother's womb. What can he know of the trees and birds outside?) Harps, streets of gold, the music of angelic choirs—these evoke a sense of splendor and beauty and peace. But they are not a street plan of heaven. Grinning devils, pitchforks, and sulphur can suggest the hideousness of hell, but they do not necessarily correspond to anything the candid camera would record. To be in heaven is to be with God forever. To be in hell is to turn your back on him forever. That is all we can know for sure until we arrive at one destination or the other.

Where are heaven and hell? Perhaps *where* doesn't make any sense. It may be that heaven and hell aren't *anywhere*, as we understand space; perhaps both exist in a kind of "fourth dimension," and the dead (now living) are all about us but not confined by space as we are. However, this is the sort of speculation you get in science fiction tales. There is no certain answer. The details are in the hands of God.

Most people are willing to leave these technical matters to God; but, as we have seen, their natural kindness revolts at the idea of anyone's going to hell. They don't want to think of God as a vengeful judge. "If God is both good and all-powerful," they say, "he would save everybody. If he doesn't save everybody, either he isn't good or he isn't all-powerful."

It is true that God is good, and that he is all-powerful. His power is such that he is able to create beings who can freely love him, or defy him. This achievement is a far more astonishing demonstration of power than would have been the manufacture of dutiful puppets. God gave us freedom, and what he gives he does not take back. Otherwise, the gift would have been a fraud from the start. We are free for eternity. And our freedom to go to heaven is not real unless we are also free to go to hell.

If you have ever taught your younger brother to drive a car, you can understand what this means. A moment comes when you must let him venture into city traffic alone. You are no longer at his side to grab the wheel or slam on the brakes. He must deal with each emergency as it arises. The whole thing is a calculated risk—he may kill himself or kill others; but unless you are willing to turn him loose he can never become a good driver.

God has a reason for giving us freedom. He wants us for his sons. Puppets cannot be sons. The love between father and sons cannot be manufactured. It comes, if it comes at all, out of freedom. In a marionette show, Romeo kisses Juliet, but there is no love in their wooden hearts.

No one has to go to hell. Hell is God's last act of love to people who will accept nothing else at his hands. He leaves them one corner of the universe which they can call their own, and in which they can continue through all eternity to live as though he did not exist.

If you go to hell, do you stay there forever? The main Christian tradition has answered in the affirmative. Day by day, our decisions, thoughts, and actions add up to a ticket stamped with one destination or the other. After death we discover what name is on the ticket. But at all stages of Christian history there have been dissenting voices, protesting that God's love is all-enduring, and that he will never cease his effort to win every last being to him. Perhaps even in hell he is at work, and one by one the souls there are wooed out of their self-imposed loneliness and selfishness.

But we dare not assume that every last soul responds to the wooer. The ability to meet love with love can atrophy, if never used. We have all known people so self-centered that no kindness or friendship could pierce the armor of their isolation. Perhaps there is a point of no return, when atrophy is complete, and hell remains certain and eternal. All we can be certain of is that God's purpose is the salvation of everybody who does not flatly refuse the offer. But he is dealing with men and women, not marionettes, and he will not ride roughshod over their freedom.

Another misgiving about Christianity, which also arises from kindness of heart, is the problem of suffering and evil. How can a loving and merciful—and all-powerful—God permit wars, murders, disease, insanity, earthquakes, and the bloody struggle of tooth and fang?

This is the question that Job asked; and it is very much in the minds and on the lips of college students. One girl summed it up briefly:

I think that there is perhaps one point upon which nearly everyone is undecided. That one is, "How does the situation in which the world now finds itself correspond to the Bible's saying, 'And God saw everything that he had made, and, behold, It was very good'?" It is impossible in our minds to reconcile ourselves to this faith, while sense evidence testifies so strongly to the contrary.

Let us put the cards on the table. No one, Christian or otherwise, knows the whole answer to this question. Christianity does not pretend to. It recognizes evil as a brute fact; it offers the insight and strength to deal with it and not be overcome. It does *not* provide a philosophic blueprint of the ultimate origin of every type of evil.

However, there are a few preliminary things that can be said with certainty. First of all, evil and suffering become an agonizing problem once you believe in three things: (1) God exists. (2) He is all-powerful. (3) He is good. By leaving out any one of these statements you can evade the problem.*

If there is no God, then you have no reliable yardstick by which to measure good and evil, so that the words are drained of meaning.

If God is good but not all-powerful, you can become a dualist and believe that your good God is opposed by an evil God equal to him in might, and that they struggle eternally without a clearcut decision. This relieves your God of any responsibility for evil. But it also destroys the meaning of evil. What right have you to say that the outlook of the "evil God" is less desirable than that of the "good God"? Both are an eternal part of the order of things; evil is therefore as natural as good. To prefer one to the other is as irrational as to like green instead of purple.

Or you can deny that our ideas of good and evil correspond to anything in God. Make him "beyond good and evil." The cancer which brings a lingering death to a young mother then becomes one tiny part of the total perfection of God's universe, as God sees it, just as a dark smudge of paint in a picture may set off the clear yellows and whites. We see so small a part of the picture that we are not competent to judge the masterpiece.

Christianity rejects these three evasions of the challenge. It says that evil is real, real in the way that a rotten egg is real. A rotten egg is a good egg gone bad. Evil is a corruption of good. If there were nothing good in the universe, there

---

* My treatment of evil and suffering agrees in general with that of G. B. Caird in *The Truth of the Gospel*, Chapter V.

could be nothing evil. The greater the good, the more poten-
tiality for evil! If an ordinary man develops a vicious streak,
he beats his wife and kicks stray puppies. Only a man with
magnificent possibilities for leadership and greatness can become a Hitler.

Evil can be broken down into three types: moral evil, pain,
and natural evil. It is a question whether natural evil—floods,
tornadoes, etc.—should be regarded as wholly bad. It may
sound belatedly Victorian to speak of life as a training in
character, but suppose that it is. Each of us has constant op-
portunities to shape himself into the sort of person he wants
to be. Too soft an environment would be an insufficient training ground. An occasional earthquake or flood may not be too
high a price for the chance to discover and practice the
courage and self-sacrifice latent within us.

But how far should this argument be pushed? It is sometimes difficult to believe that rattlesnakes are merely a stimulat-
ing part of the environment, and volcanoes a school for character. Perhaps some portion of what appears to us as natural
evil may be the reshuffling of stage scenery as God carries out
projects too vast for us to perceive. But there are moments
when things seem piled on so thick that we recall the ancient
tradition of an evil power—a "fallen angel" who amuses himself by corrupting the good world that God made. We can
say with confidence that some of the things we call natural
evil are actually wholesome goads and stimulation; but no
one knows where the boundary runs, and what or who is at
work beyond it.

The same uncertainty exists with the problem of pain. Up
to a certain point, pain is very good indeed. The man who
accidentally sticks his hand into a fire has reason to rejoice
at the existence of pain: he draws his hand back before it is

burned to the bone. Even the most extreme and prolonged kinds of pain have a curious ambivalence: one cancer victim becomes a whining, pitiful wreck; another seems to grow more tranquil and aware of God as the pain increases.

But it is cold-blooded to write of pain in this detached way. Whatever good may come of it, it becomes the terror that lies in wait for us and the dread ally of the dictators with their torture chambers. And the thing that troubles us most about pain is that there seems to be little connection between the way it is distributed and the way it ought to be distributed. Good people get killed in accidents, and wicked ones live to a lusty old age.

To remember that Christianity has never been ruggedly in-dividualistic is a help. It teaches that what affects one human being affects all. A new baby is not the exclusive joy of the two parents: the joy is shared by a large circle of relatives and friends. A bedridden invalid does not suffer alone: some-times those who love him most go through an agony as great as his, though not the same kind. But after all this has been said, there still seems to be a disproportion in the allotment of pain; and the problem would be a tormenting one indeed if we had to believe that all accounts are settled and the books balanced between the obstetrician and the mortician.

The one kind of evil that is wholly bad is moral evil. The only good that you can say about it is that it is the price we pay for freedom. We have seen that God created us with the power of choice, which means that we can make wrong deci-sions as well as right ones. Mankind as a whole has chosen to ignore or rebel against God, so that the infection of evil ex-ists in our society. We can battle against the infection, or we can add our own share of individual evil to the heritage.

The man who carelessly exposes himself to a disease falls

sick; and because of his carelessness an epidemic may spread through the city. The man who defies the "natural law" embedded in human life courts disaster, for himself and for those who stand near by. On any campus you can see how one ugly rumor, started by a single student, can quickly poison half a dozen relationships.

The effects of moral evil are like a plague, moving from city to city. But we are not helpless against it. There are methods of counterattack, vaccines that will stop its advance. The sick people can be brought back to health, if they are willing to make the attempt.

The strength of Christianity is that it begins with a God who has personal knowledge of suffering and evil. In the person of Christ, he encountered the savagery and hatred of the world; his agony on the cross links him with all tormented and tortured men and women. Whatever any of us experience, God has already experienced. If we are willing to counterattack—even though we may be raw recruits—we know that our leader is a veteran: he has come through all this himself; he knows how to give us the extra strength and wisdom to face evil and suffering head on, and come out on the other side.

Meanwhile, anyone can see that the vast bulk of evil does not stem from rattlesnakes, and tidal waves, and hurricanes. It comes from individual men and women. So the place to start working on the problem of evil is in your own heart and thoughts. This is part of the curtly practical spirit of Christianity. No matter how agreeably we may stray through pastures of speculation, exploring the unanswerable questions, it brings us back to the one person for whom we have immediate responsibility. The counterattack must begin with us.

II

CHRISTIAN REASONS FOR NOT BEING A CHRISTIAN

SOME CHRISTIANS ARE THE BEST ARGUMENT AGAINST Christianity. Here are five statements that are made time and time again when Christianity is being debated:

(1) There are lots of hypocrites in the churches.

(2) Christians are a thin-lipped crew, and never have any fun.

(3) The churches are tied in with the political and economic status quo.

(4) Christians live by blind faith and are afraid to look real facts in the face.

(5) If Christians really meant business, they would combine all the denominations into one church.

This is a serious bill of indictment. It is serious for two reasons. You can find a fair amount of evidence for all the charges. And the charges themselves stem from the teachings of the only person qualified to pass judgment: the man who founded Christianity.

The charges are worth examining one at a time, to see why

they are important. Take hypocrisy first. Here is the indictment one girl drew up:

Christianity is hypocritical. The "pillars" of the Church may well be the oldest, most dogmatic of its members. Each Sunday the pews are crowded with "worshipers" who seek personal gain by appealing to a remote power who doesn't seem too real. They nod in assent as the preacher bellows of some long-ago happening and fail to connect it with anything but that hour in church.

This is strong language; but it is gentle compared to what Christ had to say about some of the Pharisees in Palestine, who were commonly regarded as the moral leaders of the nation. Many of them actually were. Others only thought they were. It was to these self-deceivers that Christ spoke in the twenty-third chapter of Matthew:

Woe unto you, scribes and Pharisees, hypocrites! for ye devour widows' houses, and for a pretence make long prayer: therefore ye shall receive the greater damnation. . . . Ye blind guides, which strain at a gnat, and swallow a camel . . . Woe unto you, scribes and Pharisees, hypocrites! for ye are like unto whited sepulchres, which indeed appear beautiful outward, but are within full of dead men's bones, and of all uncleanness. Even so ye also outwardly appear righteous unto men, but within ye are full of hypocrisy and iniquity.

So if you know some hypocrites and double talkers in your church back home, and you don't like it, you have Christ on your side.

But the charge of sourness and lack of joy is heard even more frequently. One student put it simply:

Many of my friends who belong to a very strict church wonder why they're forbidden to dance, smoke, and have a good time in general. Why were they created if they weren't to enjoy life? You can be good and still have fun.

Another stated with acid finality:

From the outside there seems to be a singular lack of laughter connected with Christianity. Of my friends who profess to be Christians I only ask to be left alone—and I shall leave them alone and we all shall be happy.

Now a Christian can be joyless if he insists upon it, but he cannot distort Jesus into his model. Christians who really follow their leader have always scandalized sensible and earnest people by something close to lightheartedness and frivolity. They have a way of living for the day and not making jittery preparations for the morrow; they are less receptive to the sales talk of the insurance agent. And in their joy and spontaneity they have Christ for their model. He and his disciples caused many serious eyebrows to be raised. We read of Christ at dinner parties (not always with the right people), and on one occasion, when the gaiety at a wedding seemed in danger of coming to a premature end, he provided an additional supply of wine. He also promised that whoever followed him should have life and have it more abundantly.

Christ was a scandal and paradox to his virtuous contemporaries, and he still is whenever he is taken seriously. On the one hand he says, "Take up your cross and follow me," and adds stern injunctions about leaving any defective arms and eyes behind. But there is no beetle-browed heaviness about him. He has a sharp wit and sense of humor which even the beauties of the King James translation cannot obscure, and a tenderness and a playfulness which sweeten his sternest commands.* If some church people are oversolemn and act like kill-joys it is because they are imperfect imitators of their master.

* Christ's gaiety and humor are brought out especially well in Dorothy L. Sayers's cycle of radio plays, *The Man Born to Be King*.

This is true also of Christians, and there are a fair number, who value religion as a bulwark of the status quo or a kind of soothing syrup to keep people contented with things as they are. The homing instinct which guides respectable and conservative people into respectable and conservative churches, where they frequently become ruling elders or vestrymen, has long been obvious to observers. Karl Marx did not invent the phrase, "the opium of the people." It was coined by Charles Kingsley, a British clergyman, who wanted the churches to wake people up, not put them to sleep.

Every social class likes to claim Jesus as one of its own. During the Middle Ages the Church was too chummy with the lord of the manor. Protestantism, on the whole, has tended to regard the middle class as God's elect. Perhaps in the future there will be a palace revolution, and the labor unions will dominate the churches. This would be equally bad.

The Church should never sprinkle holy water over any political or economic system in its entirety, nor should it ever become the permanent and uncritical ally of any social class. All social systems are temporary. Christianity is vitally concerned with tackling the specific social problems of each time and place. Today, for example, international cooperation and the struggle for racial equality are two of the obvious priorities in Christian social action. But any alliance with particular social movements ought to be for specific purposes and a limited period of time, where there happens to be an overlapping of goals. The Kingdom of God cannot be equated with Free Enterprise, Communism, Americanism, or Democracy; nor does any social class have a monopoly of virtue and love.

However, it cannot be denied that Christ took an especially dim view of the moneyed interests. He does not appear to have done this in the spirit of a modern equalitarian, who wants to take from the rich and give to the poor. He was filled with compassion for the wealthy. He knew how hard it was for that camel to get through the needle's eye. A rich man labors under more severe temptations than almost anyone else. A rich saint—and there are some—has to overcome obstacles that would keep most of us from applying for admission to the Kingdom of God.

No one social class ought to have a dominant influence in the churches; but in actual practice the hand that signs the biggest checks often pulls the strings, so that the gospel preached Sunday after Sunday is safe and undisturbing. This is as bad as the critics of the Church say it is. The true function of a preacher is to disturb the comfortable and to comfort the disturbed.

Actually, Christ was a revolutionary; but his revolution cuts across or undercuts the familiar lines of social struggle. The Kingdom which he established, and which is visible in sudden flashes, is one in which a transformation takes place in the human heart. Love crowds out "me first." The question then becomes not "What can I grab from where?" but "What do my brothers need that I can do for them or give to them?"

All other revolutions are partial. At most, they make the have-nots into the haves, and the haves into the have-nots. Christ's kind of revolution, though very partially accomplished (the heart is stubborn), has already changed the face of the western world. The tradition of "social service," the sense of obligation toward the helpless and the underprivileged, springs from this revolution. But it is still in its early stages.

A more deeply disturbing charge is that Christianity is

afraid of truth. There is no sense in becoming a Christian unless you believe it is *true*. But, if it is true, why does it need to fear any other kind of truth?

There was the Scopes trial in Dayton, Tennessee, during the mid-1920's, when a high-school teacher was haled into court for teaching the theory of evolution. The law he had violated was one put on the statute books at the demand of certain religious groups, which wanted to protect their interpretation of Genesis from any difficult questions. Then there are the lists of forbidden books prepared by ecclesiastical authorities, to protect the innocence of the faithful.

Still darker records can be found by combing the past. Too often Christianity seems to have defended itself not by open debate in the market place but by thumbscrew and faggot. No wonder that one student grimly wrote:

The bloodiest deeds ever done by men were committed in the name of religion . . . and still are: religious intolerance, etc. I hesitate to associate myself with such an organization.

This comment is, of course, an exaggeration. In recent times, the Nazis and Communists have practiced torture and murder on a scale compared to which the Spanish Inquisition and the witch huntings of early New England were the work of amateurs. But the record is bad enough.

Two contradictory motives are probably involved in the use of strong-arm methods to save people's souls. Often the persecutor is inwardly uncertain of his own faith, and the sight of a cheerful heretic stirs his own misgiving. He puts his personal doubts at rest by disposing of the heretic. But the recourse to violence can also arise from misguided zeal—the fanatically convinced believer agonizes so greatly over his neighbor's soul that, for the sake of the soul, he is willing to do cruel things to the neighbor's body.

Baser motives play a part in the case of many persecutors. They are connected with an organization, and the power of that organization is threatened by the growth of heresy and doubt. Rationalization comes easy; the persecutor thinks he is solicitous of the unbeliever's soul, but he is actually worried about the vested interests of his own group. Pride and fear and self-interest ask nothing better than to be enveloped in the mantle of piety and true religion.

Whatever the motives, any use of coercion is plainly and blasphemously contrary to everything that Christ stood for. He never suggested that unbelievers be gagged or that the faithful wear pious blinders; he was ready to take on all comers in open debate. The way to win the skeptical and doubtful is by love, example, and peaceful persuasion—the methods of Christ. These are more powerful than all the torture chambers and faggots in creation.

The dark pages of Christian history are open for all to read. There is no excuse for them. They simply illustrate the human capacity for self-deception. But any summing up will reveal that the bright pages are more numerous. It was the Church and its monasteries that preserved classical philosophy and literature during the time of burning cities and tramping armies called the Dark Ages; preserved them and used them in the building of a new civilization which flowered in the twelfth and thirteenth centuries. Science itself has grown almost entirely on Christian soil, and often with devout Christians, such as Newton, as its pioneers. In our own country, the great majority of early schools and colleges were founded by Churches. In the average church-related college today a professor is freer to preach Relativism and Scientism than a professor in a state university is free to preach Christianity.

God is truth. Men see that truth in fragments, but the same God guides all seekers, whether they know it or not. Christianity, with all its waverings and human distortions, has endured and grown for two thousand years; it is a living religion, constantly enriched by its contacts with a widening universe. This process will continue. Whatever bit of truth is found by any man, atheist or Christian, can only deepen and enrich the faith of men and women who have given themselves to Christ.

Finally, there is the charge of sectarianism—that Christians complacently crawl off into denominational cubbyholes and lose any feeling for the larger fellowship. Here is the way one college man put it:

I often hesitate to accept Christianity because of the attitude some people take when the subject of religion comes up. Although believing in one God, they argue as to the best way to worship him. I don't appreciate the way a member of a certain religion attacks another belief. Many people I know don't have any consideration for individuals of another religion; and, in talking about the latter, they make it known through words just how they feel about them. . . . And yet, they're all supposed to be "good" Christians, and they call themselves just that.

There are more pros and cons about this accusation than any of the others. Denominationalism is not an unmixed evil. Each denomination is a kind of spiritual specialization. The Methodists are strong on social action; the Roman Catholics, Eastern Orthodox, and Anglicans, on the sacraments; the Quakers, on group mysticism and work for peace. The Presbyterians have a peculiarly vivid sense of the sovereignty of God; the Unitarians, of the possibilities of man.

If the strong points of each denomination can be poured

into one universal Church, fine. But it is better to retain the present denominations than to merge them into a vague Church which would be strong in nothing.

And yet, that answer does not satisfy. Once more, the only person qualified to speak with authority has spoken, in one of his last recorded prayers for his disciples: "That they all may be one; as thou, Father, art in me, and I in thee, that they also may be one in us: that the world may believe that thou hast sent me. And the glory which thou gavest me I have given them; that they may be one, even as we are one." (John 17:21–22.)

The present denominations are trustees to safeguard and develop the particular treasures that each can pour into the universal Church when the time comes. The moment will not arrive day after tomorrow, but large parts of the Christian world are moving in that direction. The denominational back-biting mentioned in the student quotation is on the way out. The degree of cooperation between different denominations is far greater than most people realize; infinitely greater than fifty years ago. There have been a number of mergers already; others are in the negotiation stage; the National and the World Council of Churches are powerful forces, bringing Christians of many different churches closer together. All this is not enough, but it is much more than anyone could have hoped for a hundred years ago.

We have looked at the five charges. They contain large chunks of truth. Hypocrisy, joylessness, reaction, obscurantism, and sectarianism, all exist in the churches; and, in so far as they exist, the churches and their members fall short of what Christ demands.

Does this mean that you must choose one or the other of two alternatives—that Christianity is a fine ideal but doesn't work, so you'd best leave it alone; or that Christianity is inevitably corrupted by church life, and the real Christian must go it alone?

These alternatives are too simple. But to understand why, we need to consider a couple of preliminary matters.

In the first place, if some of the most deadly evils are found inside the Christian fellowship, that is exactly what we should expect. "Lilies that fester smell far worse than weeds," Shakespeare drily observed. And if there is some force of evil in the universe—call it the Devil or whatever you will—we can be sure that it is constantly trying to turn Christians into hypocrites, stuffed shirts, and enemies of love and truth. Sometimes it succeeds.

But we can't blame everything on the prince of darkness. A second thing to consider is this: as we look at the conventional Christians in the church down the street, many of them appear lukewarm, insincere, or even vicious. But we can't know what they would be like if their small portion of faith disappeared altogether. They might be much worse.

Some people seem to be born relatively kind and helpful, whereas others have more than their share of the old Adam. It is no accident that notorious sinners—murderers and drunkards and sexual deviants—so often turn to religion. They *know* that they need some outside power to keep them from going completely on the rocks. Thus it is that in Alcoholics Anonymous the newcomers must be taught to rely on God if they want to stop relying on the bottle.

An atheist, blessed with a sturdy digestion and a sunny disposition, may look better to the impartial observer than a Christian all twisted up inside. But the important point is which way the two men are going. Maybe the atheist is gradually hardening into permanent complacency and self-admiration. Maybe the Christian, who seems so short-tempered and nasty, is inching a bit nearer to the final mystery of love.

So far we have been engaged in passing judgment on the people around us. It is a pleasant game, but the results aren't very accurate. We are looking at people from the outside. Only God can see them from the inside.

What does all this add up to? A challenge. If you believe that Christ is let down by his professed followers, you ought to be in the thick of things. This means belonging to a church and being active in it. It means being willing to speak up as a Christian in even the most emancipated bull session and fraternity circles. It means having a sharp eye for sub-Christian practices and attitudes on the campus. (Is cheating condoned —are you doing anything about it?)

It strikes me that we had better stop this Olympian detachment and come down to ourselves. I once amused myself by drawing up an "examination of conscience" slanted toward college professors. When I tried to answer the questions I didn't feel very happy. Here are some of them that I recall: Have I ever given an evasive answer when a student asked me a question in class? Have I ever been influenced by personalities in marking papers? In my scholarly writing, have I ever skimmed lightly over facts that would contradict a point I was trying to make?

Several undergraduates, who prefer to remain anonymous, have kindly drawn up a similar list for students. They started with the assumption that sincerity and fair play are virtues almost universally cherished on the campus, and could be used as twin yardsticks. Here are their questions:

1. Have I ever dated someone not because of personal liking, but for the prestige involved?
2. When I joined a fraternity or sorority, did I choose it be-

cause I liked its members, or because it was the outfit with the most prestige?

3. Do I ever cheat on exams or term papers?

4. Do I ever polish the apple?

5. Do I keep silent in class because I'm afraid other students will think I'm a long-haired intellectual?

6. Do I invent imaginary reasons for needing more money when I write to my parents?

7. Do I ever get drunk because I'm afraid the crowd will think me a sissy if I don't?

8. Do I talk about other students behind their backs?

If you study this list, and other questions you can think up for yourself, I think you will experience some interesting psychological phenomena. All sorts of good reasons will spring up in your mind to "explain" any admissions you have to make. The attempt at self-evaluation is such a severe discipline that if you try to do a thorough job you really don't have much time and energy left for rating your fellow students or fellow Christians.

Christianity is medicine, and the Church is a hospital. Both are for hypocrites, double-talkers, and phonies like you and me. The one big difference between a genuine Christian and anybody else is that the Christian is sick and knows it; everybody else is sick and thinks he is well.

The course of treatment is lifelong. But there are two things we can be sure of: We shall have plenty of companionship with our fellow patients all along the way. And the physician is absolutely reliable.

12

FITTING THE JIGSAW PUZZLE TOGETHER

COLLEGE YEARS ARE A TIME FOR BEING INTELLIGENTLY unhappy. Growing up is always agonizing. The more you mature in college, the less your days will be the rollicking, carefree ones that you saw in the movies of college life when you were in high school.

Possibly you brought a real religion to college, and it has kept pace with your growth. If so, count yourself lucky. Far more likely, your faith has eroded away inch by inch as the waves of doubt and skepticism beat against it in classroom, laboratory, and bull session.

Even though your mind may tell you, "I'm glad to be rid of this old stuff," something else in you feels the emptiness as earlier certainties dissolve and leave nothing firm in their place. Not that the erosion is necessarily bad—for the time being. It clears the ground for the new freedom, which we examined in an earlier chapter.

The campus offers you this wider freedom. Now that you have it, you begin to discover its dangers and responsibilities.

Suppose you organize an expedition to filch copies of a forthcoming exam, and your buddy happens to be the one who is detected and summoned to the dean's office. What are you going to do? You can keep quiet and feel like a traitor. Or you can speak up and face the dean with your friend. Freedom in itself cannot tell you what to do. You begin to wish that you had some sort of road map to guide you through the land of freedom.

Or imagine this common situation: A girl and boy have a quarrel, and she returns his fraternity pin. After a few days her anger dies down and she wants him back again. But she is too proud to say so, and he is too proud to take the first step. It's a stalemate. At this point she can resort to the classical ruse, cast friendly looks at another boy and start going with him, in the well founded hope that boy friend number one will be jealous enough to leap back into the field. But should she? Is it fair to use another human being as a decoy, then drop him cold after he has served his purpose?

A complete Machiavellian wouldn't worry about these questions. But there aren't many Machiavellians. Most people want to be at peace with themselves. So again, there is the desire for definite guidance. You have freedom, but what are you going to do with it?

Experiences like these lead to the discovery of the "we-group"—or rather, its rediscovery. There is a rhythm about this. The we-group is discovered and rediscovered throughout life. The newborn baby is the family's center of gravity, but year by year he is taught that, no matter how great his charms, he is only one part of that bigger thing, the family. With his arrival in the teens, the "I" demands new liberties and honors. The mold of family living has to be broken, so that "I" can grow. "I" goes to college. And then the whole thing must be done all over again, as the liberated "I" encounters a new we-group. Again a balance of power is painfully achieved. Still later, after graduation, the process is repeated once more, as "I" adjusts to work and marriage.

The discovery or rediscovery of the we-group, and the perplexing responsibilities that ensue, are often sufficient to set anyone on the quest for some clear practical guidance. This doesn't necessarily mean going religious. A common-sense code of conduct, to keep all the "I's" from bruising one another, may be the modest goal.

But even this limited search has a way of leading by tiny stages to a search for God, because he turns out to be the only firm basis for a code of conduct based on anything stronger than minute-by-minute expediency.

In yet another way, God often creeps up on you when you are least expecting him. He works through your intellectual confusion—the questions you ask that receive no satisfactory answers, in courses, or casual conversations. The confusion is likely to get worse before it gets better. One coed expressed it with a touch of desperation:

The whole thing is that college students are confused about everything in this world, and religion is one of them. I just hope we can get straightened out.

The secular gods—Progress, Humanitarianism, Scientism, etc.—will do for a time, but they leave too many blank spaces. Out of confusion comes a desire for a really complete way of looking at life and the universe, a way that will satisfy both the mind and the heart. (You are born with both.) You want to see all partial truths fall together into one big truth, and you want the big truth to be one you can serve and love.

God is also working you over in experiences that you still

remember with anguish when your own children are ready for college. The cribbing that was detected, your betrayal of friends, the sudden realization "I've been a complete heel"— these are moments of the dark depths, and God is an expert fisherman.

Sometimes, indeed, it seems that he rubs your face in the muck, causing you to loathe yourself and feel as though a nest of copperheads were inside your heart. This is his shock treatment, to make you realize that any purely common-sense code of living decently and managing your own life is beyond your strength. By revealing your weakness, the weakness of everybody, he hopes to make you cry out for a strength greater than your own.

But God also woos, though the wooer is seldom recognized by name. He woos when you have an intense feeling, usually very brief, that "time is standing still" and the whole universe is frozen into living perfection. This may come while you are listening to music or making love or solving a difficult math problem or walking across campus on the way to the gym. You cannot shake off the memory. Nor can you relive it at will. The experience comes unbidden, which is when you least expect it. It is actually a hint or sample or shadow of a particular sort of life known in theological language as the "life everlasting."

As these experiences—problems of conduct, intellectual confusion, dark moments, and luminous moments—mount up, you begin to feel the hot breath of pursuit on the nape of your neck. If a bull session on religion is going on, you can't keep away from it; but your questions have a strident edge. When you pick up a book like this one, you quite properly give it the fine-tooth-comb treatment, intent on spotting any careless statements of fact or loose-jointed logic. And when you find some examples, as you are certain to do, you have a sense of liberation for a little while: the breath is no longer hot on your neck.

But the sense of being pursued and wooed soon returns. Someone is close behind you, and you know it, no matter how you resist the feeling. Do you want to continue the flight, or turn around and decide you will acknowledge the pursuer?

If you feel a pull toward one of the sciences, you don't spend your time chatting with people about the pros and cons of the scientific method. You go into the laboratory and set to work on the basic experiments. By this means you discover whether you want to be a scientist.

If you feel the unmistakable presence of God, there are experiments you can perform, to determine whether you are ready to welcome him into your life. You can turn your life into a laboratory, with yourself as both the experiment and the observer.

Suppose you set yourself a six months' experiment. It involves no closing of your eyes. If you have doubts, take them along with you. Your laboratory experiment might be set up like this:

(1) Fence in fifteen minutes each day for reading the Bible. Start with any of the gospels (my own suggestion would be Luke or John), but read all of them before you are through. You may want to read through one gospel rather quickly, then on other days take it more slowly, perhaps a chapter at a time. See what picture of Christ builds up in your mind. Do not try to force the picture into any particular form, and do not try to fight against the picture as it gradually forms.

(2) Set aside another fifteen minutes each day for prayer. If you feel like a hypocrite, you can preface your prayers

with "God, if there is a God . . ." Keep silent at least half of the time, and quietly try to clear your mind of the eighteen hundred stray thoughts that will keep creeping in. Pray for understanding, for intellectual honesty. Pray for friends who are in difficulty. If you feel grateful for something, or have glimpses of insight into God's greatness and love, tell him so. (Prayer is so extremely important a part of this experiment that you will need either a good adviser, or some simple book on the subject. Several excellent ones are listed in Appendix B.)

(3) Go to church somewhere every Sunday. Do not focus your attention primarily on the sermon. It may be dull or stupid. Go to church not to argue with the preacher or with yourself, but to worship—still in the spirit of "God, if there is a God," if that is how you feel.

(4) Do your best day by day to live according to the teachings of Christ. For present purposes, this means, "Love everybody in the same way you love yourself; treat the persons around you the way that love demands." (You will find that you fail time and again. If you take the failures seriously they will be very valuable, because they will throw you back more strongly toward God, who alone is able to make this kind of living possible.)

You can attend bull sessions forever, ask countless questions during Religious Emphasis Week, and read a stack of books like this one; but nothing will come of it unless you get at least your toes wet in the water that laps at your feet.

But before making even this cautious experiment, you want to know whether the credentials of Christianity can stand up to honest examination, and what the word Christianity means as used by the great majority of Christians. The final two chapters will attempt to answer these questions.

13

THE CREDENTIALS OF CHRISTIANITY

We have looked at the arguments against Christianity. Many of them, solidly intellectual at first glance, have turned out to be emotional. The rational mind is friendly to faith, but the nervous system revolts. It doesn't relish the absolute commitment demanded by real belief in God.

We have cleared a path through the mine field; but mine clearing is a negative operation. Now, at last, we can go forward a few yards and examine the positive credentials of Christianity.

First, one thing must be bluntly said. No religion can be "proved" in the way that a mathematical equation can be proved. This is not a problem unique to religion. The way to prove college is to go to college; the way to prove the profession of law is to become a lawyer. Of course you don't plunge ahead blindly. You study the college catalogue and talk with alumni before you sign up at Maplecrest or Gargantua; you read vocational manuals and converse with experienced lawyers before you dedicate yourself to law. Then, if everything seems to point in one direction, you commit your-self: by enrolling in college or choosing law for your career. Only afterward can you be sure that you have chosen wisely.

The public evidence for Christianity is of three main kinds. To begin with, there is its very peculiar history. We can un-derstand how Mohammedanism spread. Territory for its mis-sionary growth was carved out by flashing scimitars. And Communism, a religion in fact if not in name, has expanded by meeting hate with hate, intrigue with intrigue, violence with violence.

Christianity's early history is very strange. It won an Empire through gentleness and nonresistance. For almost three hun-dred years Christianity had no official status in the Roman Empire. During most of that time, membership in the Church was a criminal offense. Widespread and incredibly brutal per-secutions were constantly unleashed. The Christians did not fight violence with violence. They blessed their tormenters; they prayed for the men who released wild animals and lighted the faggots. The blood of the martyrs was truly the seed of the Church. It is as though an irresistible force wore down all opposition. An Empire was conquered, not by swords and tramping armies, but by unflinching faith and steady love.

In the second place, the saints are visible evidence that the Holy Spirit—God within—has been at work throughout Chris-tian history. When we read Socrates' last conversation with his friends, while the jailor stood outside preparing the cup of hemlock, we are moved by a sense of absolute nobility. But the Christian saints at their best, such as Francis and Brother Lawrence and Albert Schweitzer, have a quality not found in even the greatest of the ancient Greeks. There is something luminous about them; the Light shines through them. With all their sharply individual traits, with all their imperfections (which they would be the first to acknowledge), they are none the less mirrors held up to Christ. In them we see his unbroken chain of witnesses.

However, the third type of evidence is the easiest to discuss systematically. Almost everyone owns a Bible. How good are its credentials?

People talk of the Bible as though it were one book. Actually it is a library. It was written by dozens of authors over about a thousand years. All the same, it has unity. It is an interpretation of history, with God as the central character. There are so many subplots that the reader easily goes astray on side paths, but the main outline of the story is simple. An hourglass shape will accurately diagram it:

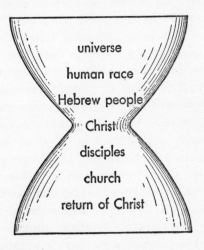

In other words, the Bible begins with the account, in highly symbolic language, of God's creation of the universe and its different forms of life. Then the human race, poetically telescoped into Adam and Eve, appears on the scene. Soon the story narrows down. The spotlight is turned on one small fraction of mankind, the Hebrew people, which God has singled out for a unique purpose. Most of the Old Testament is devoted to their history.

At the beginning of the New Testament, the spotlight focuses upon one solitary figure: Christ. But when he begins his ministry other figures come into the widening circle of light. These are his disciples. After a few years they spread out into the Roman Empire; and their successors penetrate into practically every part of the world. The Church, expanding through space and time, represents the broadening out of the hourglass toward the bottom.

But the Church is not the ultimate goal. It is one of the agencies through which God's will is worked out. We live in an interim period. In the "fullness of time" God, acting through Christ, will bring about the culmination of history, radically transforming the world. The Kingdom of God, which we now experience in part, will become a solid and eternal reality. So the Bible points beyond itself toward a future, however distant, in which God's will is perfectly done.

But—getting back to an earlier part of the story—wasn't it unfair of God to play favorites? Why did he choose the Hebrews instead of the Javanese or the Eskimos?

Unfair or not, this is the way that real things happen. The telephone was invented by Alexander Graham Bell at Boston in 1876. Radium was discovered in France by the Curies in 1898. Both are now the property of the whole world, but each was discovered or invented somewhere in particular.

Though God did pick out the Hebrews for his special revelation, no real favoritism was involved. A college student laboring late into the night to pass his premedical course is not pampered. He is being trained so that he may be useful to other people. God might have chosen the Javanese or the Eskimos, but he happened to select the Hebrews; and he trained them so that they might share with the whole world the special things he taught them.

The Hebrews paid a stiff price for this responsibility. They were always being overrun by more powerful neighbors. The easy, comfortable thing would have been to intermarry with their pagan overlords, worship the local gods, and cease to exist as a separate people. They would probably have done so if they hadn't been convinced that God wanted them to keep their separate existence—as part of his plans for the benefit of the whole world.

The Old Testament, taken by itself, is a mysterious book. It hints at some coming event which will draw the loose strands of history and experience together and reveal in clear daylight the plans that God has been a long time preparing. The New Testament takes up where the Old Testament leaves off. Christ is now revealed as the culmination of all that has gone before.

The Bible is the primary source book of Christian belief. If anyone could prove that it is a patchwork of lies and old wives' tales, Christianity would dissolve into the mists of mythology, and take its place on the library shelf alongside Mithraism and countless ancient cults. A great many students strongly suspect that precisely this is happening. Here are some random misgivings:

I sometimes hesitate to accept Christianity for the usual reasons. First, because of my intense belief that the Bible is made up of a number of stories, which, at least in the Old Testament, amount to a number of good moral stories but are not to be taken as factual history. The people of that time, ignorant of many forces which we now consider common, were no doubt apt to take nature's freaks as being miracles. The New Testament, although much more factual, cannot be taken without criticism. It, too, is full of loopholes and misinterpreted stories. Therefore, if you discount the Bible to any great extent, you are bound to have a feeling of hesitancy regarding Christianity.

We don't know who wrote the Bible, how much is plagiarized, how accurate the writers were, and what has been lost down through the years in translations.

These comments are echoes of what has gone on for more than a century. During that time the study of the Bible has been revolutionized. A succession of scholars, representing all shades of Christianity as well as outright skepticism, have put the entire Bible through the same merciless analysis that Beowulf, the Iliad, and the Odyssey have endured. Indeed, no book in the world has been so thoroughly squeezed through the wringer of scholarship as the Bible.

The first reports from the scholars were very disturbing to men who had thought of the Bible as an L.P. record dictated by God. Take the book of Isaiah. We now know that at least two different authors had a hand in it, and they were not contemporaries. Only one of them was the historical Isaiah. The Hebrews, possessing no copyright laws, and not esteeming originality as much as we do, did not hesitate to make additions to old books, in the spirit (they hoped) of the original writer, whose name was retained for the composite product.

The scholars also found that, while the earlier historical books represent a genuine tradition of what happened before the Hebrews conquered the Promised Land, they have been retold from the viewpoint of the later prophets. Genesis, Exodus, etc., are not straight history (if such a thing ever exists in any book) but interpreted history.

The problem of Old Testament criticism is so complicated that it cannot be considered in detail here. But the net result has been constructive, not destructive. We now have a deepened appreciation of the unique religious evolution of the Hebrews, and the unique value of the Bible as the record and interpretation of that evolution—in which God played the leading role. The older way of looking at the Bible was too mechanical and static. It obscured the personality of the flesh-and-blood men who wrote the various parts of the Bible, and submerged the plain indications of slow century-by-century growth in religious understanding. We can see, far more clearly than our forefathers could, that the Hebrews were on the anvil of a very special kind of history, and that their religious insight and depth were the product hammered out painfully, stroke by stroke.

Thanks to modern scholarship, we can also observe the Old Testament story emerging from frank myth through half-legendary history to unmistakable history. Adam and Eve are allegorical characters (the Hebrew word Adam means "man"); Abraham and his descendants hover in the twilight zone between legend and history; the flight from Egypt rings true in its broad details, though Moses appears with a nimbus of myth about his head; David is as solidly historical as President Wilson.

However, the mythological elements in the Old Testament are not excess baggage. Mythology is a kind of racial shorthand. So the particular myths which sprang up among the Hebrews or were adapted by them from other peoples are an objectification of how they looked at the world and how God appeared to them. C. S. Lewis has a very striking phrase; if the Hebrews were indeed the chosen people it is logical to believe, he argues, that their mythology was the "chosen mythology," * peculiarly adapted for dramatizing the truths that God wished to express through them.

Most skeptics are willing to grant that an admixture of legend and myth in the Old Testament is not fatal to its general import, which remains clear enough. Indeed, the mythological portions often serve effectively to state the main themes. But if the scholars could show that the New Testament is equally shot through with legendary material, and that Christ himself is nothing but a myth, the game would be up. You cannot have Christianity without a Christ.

A hundred years ago, many of the best scholars seemed to be moving in precisely this direction. As their surgical knives worked at the New Testament, peeling away layer after layer, it looked as though no core would be left.

Take the first three Gospels. Strauss, in 1835, believed they were all later than A.D. 150—that they had been written at least one hundred twenty years after the crucifixion, when the last eyewitnesses were long since underground. Baur, in 1847, was almost as extreme in his views. He suggested A.D. 130 as the date for Matthew, and 150 for Mark and Luke.

Now if the Gospels were written a hundred or more years after the time of Christ, they are practically worthless. Several generations would lie between Christ and the writers. Legends could spring up in great numbers and grow more fantastic every year, unchallenged by eyewitnesses. The question naturally arose in the nineteenth century: Did Christ ever live at all? Books were written to prove he was a sun-god or a mythological figure on the same level of reality as Isis and Osiris, the Egyptian gods. Other writers thought that someone named Jesus had indeed lived, that he was a simple Galilean peasant who did good and taught people a simple

* C. S. Lewis, *Miracles*, p. 161 n.

morality, but that somebody (usually Paul) perverted his innocent message by clothing its author in divine trappings.

The student comments which I have quoted really stem from the nineteenth century. For fifty years now the biblical scholars have been telling a very different story. They have found that you can peel away the outer layers of the New Testament, but the core is there, and it is firm to the touch. The gospels, it is now clear, are much earlier than any scholar would have believed possible a hundred years ago.

It is interesting to get an over-all picture of how most biblical scholars look at the first three Gospels today, and what dates they assign to them. (A majority of the experts would place John close to A.D. 100, but it involves so many special problems that I omit it from this discussion.) Some of the details would be disputed by this scholar or that, but there is increasing agreement about the general conclusions.

Bear in mind that Christ was crucified around A.D. 30. This will give you an idea of how much time elapsed before each of the Gospels reached its present form.

A.D. 30–50

This is the period of oral gospels. The instruction given to converts was mostly by word of mouth. Gradually, it began to assume a more fixed and definite form. Certain episodes from Christ's life and many of his parables and other teachings were memorized by evangelists and told from community to community. (We have to remember that the men of the first century were far more accustomed to memorizing than we are, and more accurate.) The oral accounts of Christ's deeds and words probably came in large part from the men who had actually known him. A great number of eyewitnesses were still alive, and would be quick to detect falsifications. Finally, toward the end of these two decades, people here and there started writing down what they knew about Christ. You can imagine a missionary jotting down the sayings of Christ in a notebook, to have them for handy reference. Definite collections of this sort began to evolve.

A.D. 50

About this time, one particular collection of Christ's teachings, supplemented by a few episodes from his life, took definite form, and was widely circulated. This booklet is what the scholars call by the neutral label of "Q," from the German word *Quelle*, source. It no longer exists as a separate document, but several of the gospel writers incorporated long portions of it into their works.

A.D. 60

A physician named Luke, who was Paul's traveling companion, decided to make a start toward a systematic account of the life and teachings of Christ. He had a copy of Q before him. He had also picked up another document while traveling with Paul in Palestine a couple of years earlier, or possibly he had jotted down information which was given to him by word of mouth. Systematic and thorough—in fact, very much like a modern research historian—Luke set about comparing the two sources of information, and perhaps some others. Very likely he began writing his gospel at this time. But if he did he remained dissatisfied with it, and made no attempt to publish it.*

---

* The theory that Luke began writing his gospel around A.D. 60 is very widely accepted, though some scholars contend that he did not begin until 80 or 85. In any case, it is clear that in his complete gospel he made use of Q, and also of some special source, probably secured in Palestine. His third main source was Mark.

A.D. 65–70

John Mark, who had also been one of Paul's traveling companions, wrote the Gospel According to St. Mark. The Jerusalem Church was accustomed to meeting at the home of Mark's mother shortly after the crucifixion. According to a very old tradition, which few scholars now question, Mark served as Peter's interpreter in Rome, presumably translating the Aramaic sermons into Greek or Latin. The same tradition says that Mark used Peter's sermons when he wrote his gospel. Internal evidence points strongly toward this. Note how vivid are the episodes in which Peter figures. Mark, of course, also utilized other sources of information; but in part his gospel appears to reflect the memories of a man who had been one of Christ's first disciples.

A.D. 80–85

Luke came on a copy of Mark's gospel, recognized its value, and incorporated large sections of it into the rough draft of the gospel he was working on. Satisfied at last, he published the work.

A.D. 85

Somebody—probably *not* Matthew the publican—wrote a gospel based on three main sources: (1) Mark; (2) Q; (3) some document or oral tradition which cannot be pinned down very definitely. The name of Matthew seems to have become attached to this gospel because of a tradition that he had compiled a collection of Jesus' sayings, but other evidence for his authorship is lacking.

Suppose that a young man of twenty had been present at the crucifixion. About the time of his fortieth birthday or a little earlier, he could have walked into a bookstore and purchased a copy of Q, to see whether it faithfully reported the teachings of Christ. In his late fifties he might have secured a copy of Mark, with its strong reflections of Peter's vivid memories. Around the time he reached the traditional three-score years and ten, editions of both Luke and Matthew would be available.

Copies of the New Testament, written on vellum, exist from the fourth century on. These early copies have many variations in phrasing, but none of crucial importance. They are substantially the same as the New Testament you hold in your hand. Fragments of much older manuscripts have recently turned up. A scrap of papyrus containing a few verses from John's gospel was acquired in 1920 by the John Rylands Library of Manchester, England; on the basis of the style of handwriting it can hardly be much later than A.D. 125.

Earlier than any of the gospels are Paul's epistles. The first of these (Galatians and 1 Thessalonians) probably date from around A.D. 50, at least fifteen years before Mark published his gospel; but the attitude Paul reveals toward Christ is essentially the same as that reflected throughout the Gospels, and he had had the opportunity to become intimately acquainted with many leaders of the Christian movement—men who had known Christ personally and could give him all the information he wished.

The evidence for the Jesus of the New Testament is as solid as the evidence for Julius Caesar. We are at liberty, if we wish, to insist that most of the details *must* be mythological additions, but we cannot call in the support of modern scholarship for this conviction. The main outlines of the gospel accounts stand very clear and firm; they have been subjected to every test that scholarship can devise, and have stood the test. If you reject them, it is because you are convinced that a person such as Jesus simply could not have lived. But this is like the little farm boy who went to the zoo, gazed long at a giraffe, and then firmly announced, "That thing *can't* be a real animal."

14

THE THREE WORDS OF CHRISTIANITY

You can think of Christianity as one road toward one goal. There are many side paths, worth exploring for their own sake. Some circle around and come back to the main road. Others are dead-end trails and demand an ultimate backtracking if you are to go where you want to go. But the main road is there for all who wish to travel, and is clearly marked.

To travel along the main road you need to understand three words. They are man, God, and love. They are the triple password to all the complexities of theology.

These three words look simple. They are monosyllables, everyday words. But the shortest words are often the most packed with meaning.

What can you say about man? First of all, that he is a bundle of extremes, contradictions, and paradoxes.

He has a body inherited from the animals, but he stands upright like a marble shaft straining for the sun. He can be crueler than any beast; he is the inventor of total war, concentration camps, torture chambers, gas chambers. His tenderness can reach out toward every living being, as when a small child restores a fallen bird to its nest or a grown man steps aside to spare the worm in his path.

He builds cities, knowing that he will not live to enjoy them. In the midst of frantic activity he sees always the skull at the banquet table. He is restless from birth. No triumph or satisfaction available on earth can satisfy him. His life is brief and is a kaleidoscope of fear, anguish, joy, impatience, and gray stretches of boredom.

This strange creature was invented and manufactured by God. The human race came into existence because God willed its existence. Over what seem to us endless expanses of time, life traveled down the assembly line of God's workshop, and man came off the moving belt.

But God did more than invent the human race. He invented it for a special purpose. He implanted certain characteristics that reflect himself. One is the power of rational thought. Another is the ability to make decisions. These two, taken together, spell freedom. A bird builds nests of a particular kind because nest building is written into its nature. But man is free to build a house, live in a cave, or sleep under the stars. Man is also free to obey God or to defy him.

Our special purpose is, with joyful free will, to become the adopted sons and daughters of God. This means that every moment in life is of cosmic and everlasting significance. By our choices, however trivial, we move away from God or toward him.

We can, if we choose, turn inward, crawl into a make-believe house, and pretend that we are the midpoint of the universe. We are free to do this, we are free to choose hell, now and forever. Hell is living forever as though God does not exist.

But we are also free, if we choose, to begin living in heaven here and now, and in time and beyond time we shall live completely in heaven, which is simply a name for being in God's naked presence.

Another thing can be said about man. He finds it extremely difficult to use his freedom well. Something inside him keeps whispering: "You are the center of creation; you are God." We are bundles of competing egos, at war with one another, at war with God. If we drift along and "do the natural thing" we more often than not travel a dead-end bypath toward complete self-centeredness and ultimate, cosmic loneliness.

But what of God? He, too, is a bundle of paradoxes, at least as we try to understand him. He is farther away and less subject to our control than the most distant stars. He is also closer to us than our eyeballs. He is hard to see, for either he is too far away or he is too near for our middle-range eyes.

If the sight of a winter sky, with its thousands and millions of stars and its immense space, can fill us with awe, the awe is still greater when we think of God, who made the entire universe and sustains it, keeps it going, day by day, second by second.

This is the awe of magnitude and power. But we feel another kind of awe in God's presence. We sense his complete goodness. "Goodness" is too pallid, too human a word. It is God's holiness, his *otherness*, that makes us feel, upon experiencing it, like Isaiah when he saw his vision of the Lord in the temple at Jerusalem. Isaiah's words express what millions have felt, in some brief and burning meeting with God: "Woe is me! for I am undone; because I am a man of unclean lips, and I dwell in the midst of a people of unclean lips: for mine eyes have seen the King, the Lord of hosts."

The ancient Hebrews experienced the majesty and might

and holiness of God before they fully perceived his gentler traits. The same order of experience is good for the individual, first approaching God. Only after we have some grasp of God's magnitude and holiness are we prepared to understand how incredible is the other side of God.

This is his closeness to us, his loving friendship. Quite literally, he numbers the hairs on each person's head and is aware of the sparrow's fall. The tiniest detail of every life is constantly present to him. And his concern is not a cold, impersonal one. It is the concern of love. God's love is even more fundamental in our thinking about him than his majesty or his holiness; but we cannot fully understand his love unless we first acknowledge his majesty and holiness.

However, if one word can come closest to describing God, that word is "love." It is his steady, unchanging, unyielding love that gives us the assurance we can come into his holy presence and not be consumed by it.

"Love" is the third of the key words. Now love has many meanings. It may mean that you are reaching for something you need. When people commonly say, "I love apple pie," they mean, "I want apple pie." The pie neither wants anything nor desires to be wanted. Or love can mean give and take. "I'll do this for you, and you do that for me." At its best, such love is a splendid and noble thing, a basis of friendship and marriage. But it is not quite what is meant by God's love.

Love, as applied to God, means giving without demanding anything in return. God loves us simply because it is his nature to love. He loves us whether we deserve it or not.

But this love is not sentimental. It must be understood in the light of God's holiness. God is not a wishful thinker. Just as he sees our latent possibilities more clearly than our neighbors, so he also discerns our inner nastiness more precisely than any psychoanalyst. He loves us not so much for what we are, but in spite of what we are. And because he loves us he does not intend to leave us as we are. His love is the torch that burns away the impurities and dross, leaving the essential "I," which he can then guide as it grows toward its fulfillment.

This kind of love is contagious. The person who has experienced it in his own meeting with God begins to find it welling up in himself. More and more, love becomes the secret of his being, and its results are visible in his dealings with other people, and his attitude toward everything from family life to civic affairs and international problems.

Love grows only when you do not try to bottle it up. It circulates like blood. God is the beating heart. The circling stream of love flows through God and all who respond to him, and it is constantly purified and strengthened at its source.

All of Christian morality is summed up in Augustine's epigram, "Love God, and then do what you want to." But only a saint could find this adequate. The Ten Commandments, the Golden Rule, the special teachings about marriage and other human situations are necessary because we need concrete guidance on how to follow the leadership of love.

But love itself is the touchstone, and the motive of all genuine Christian living. To substitute a list of rules and regulations and live according to cold duty is better than nothing; but it is less than Christ demands and offers.

Beneath all the complexities of Christian belief there is the triple password, simple enough for a child to understand and use: Man, God, and Love. But these words by themselves may resemble abstract entries in a dictionary. Is there any way they can be brought together, so that we can see them all in some living relationship and at top strength?

The answer of Christianity, the one thing that makes it unique among all the religions and philosophies of the world, is that the three words come together in one man. Jesus is fully man, fully God, and fully love.

To get a glimmering of how this can be, something must be said about the doctrine of the Trinity. The whole idea of a "threeness" within God is a result of the impact of Christ's life. In an immediate, nonintellectual way, the men and women who followed him became convinced that somehow he was "one" with God. But they knew also that he prayed to his "Father in heaven," and was constantly aware of being guided from above. So, if he was God, there must be some sort of multiplicity within God.

A little later—at Pentecost—the first disciples recognized what they called the Holy Ghost or Holy Spirit—God active within them individually and as a group. This was a third way of experiencing God. We can think of the Holy Spirit as Christ's messenger and agent in our hearts, continuously and quietly at work, remaking us, training us, preparing us, in the magnificent words of the old catechism, "to glorify God and to enjoy him for ever."

The doctrine of the Trinity is not a blueprint *explaining* the inner reality of God. It is a set of statements designed to safeguard the mystery, to keep people from explaining it away by oversimple explanations. The Trinity means that God is experienced in three different ways, which may be roughly described as God the Father (God above us), God the Son (God beside us), and God the Holy Spirit (God within us). And the doctrine goes farther—it suggests that this threefold distinction is not due merely to our human way of perceiving things. It corresponds to something within God himself. There is one God, and only one God, but he is not monolithic. Within his unity there are three centers, or "Persons," or whatever word you wish to use.

There are human analogies to give us some hint of how this could be. Dorothy L. Sayers, in her book *The Mind of the Maker*, has shown that the writing of a book involves a trinitarian process. There is first the disembodied idea of the book, in the "heaven" of the author's mind. This idea becomes incarnate when the writer sits down at his desk and converts the idea into words on sheets of paper. And when the book is published and people read it the book produces power—its effect on the reader. In theological terms, the parallels would be:

Idea   =   God the Father
Book   =   God the Son
Effect   =   God the Holy Spirit

However, no human analogy is completely satisfactory. The concept of the Trinity involves an extra "dimension." We can talk about God as the three-in-one, and find hints of confirmation in personal contacts with him, but we cannot grasp the concept in a visual way.

But if the doctrine of the Trinity is less an explanation of the mystery than a safeguarding it does illumine one other mystery that would otherwise haunt the thoughtful believer in God. Assume that God is monolithic—that the Trinity is not true. Then whom or what did he love before there was any universe to love? If the Trinity corresponds to something basic in God's own being, it is easy to see how love can also be basic in him. From all eternity, each Person of the Trinity has loved the two others, so that a circulation of love has always existed within God himself.

But we are ready now to return to Christ. The fundamental assertion is that Christ unites the three words: he is man, God, and love.

Christ was fully human. In fact, he was and is more human than you or I. Again we come to the dreary fact that each of us is distorted and scarred by sin, which is a simple word used to describe our defiance of God and all the daily consequences that flow from this and our self-centeredness. It is as though each of us bears a cancer in his body. Christ has no cancer. A cancer makes you less than human, because it does not belong in a healthy body. So in Christ we have a portrait of what every life is meant to be but is not: joyful obedience to God, love and helpfulness to the people around you. The social scientists study man as he is in his everyday actions. Christ reveals man as he is meant to be, and as God intends him to be after the cancer has been burned away.

Christ reveals human nature as it is *meant to be*. He also reveals God as God *is*. To put it in theological terms, the second Person of the Trinity became incarnate when Christ was born. Christ is God, translated into human terms. It is as though a Chinese book has been rendered into English. God is made visible by Christ, who is his translation or photograph.

Such was the gradual conviction of the plain men and women who followed Christ throughout Palestine. And the same impact of Christ continues to this day. Person after person has an experience similar to that of the disciples who knew him face to face. First there is the belief in God; but often God seems far away and hard to grasp. Then, by a flash of insight or slow growth of faith it is impossible to trace, the jump is made. Christ becomes someone to whom prayer and worship are addressed. Immediately, the concept of God is sharpened; the reality of prayer and worship, immensely increased; and there is the sense of being freed from an intolerable weight of frustration and guilt.

Christ, therefore, is both human and divine. And he is also complete love. His whole life on earth was one of loving self-giving. So the very word "love," when used in Christianity, is defined by Christ. To act with love is to act like Christ.

Christ's love was revealed throughout his life, but most dramatically and deeply in his death. By compromising a little here and a little there, by being more careful in the way he dealt with important people, he could have avoided the cross; but, at whatever inner agony (remember the Garden of Gethsemane), he chose not to avoid it. The man who, of all the men and women known to history, least deserved a criminal's death, was tortured to death between two thieves. And by his death he finished building the road between man and God.

How is this so? Each of us carries a heavy sack on his back, filled with self-centeredness, pride, and all their fruits. By the whole sweep of his life, culminating upon the cross, Christ takes upon his own shoulders the impossible weight we are not strong enough to bear. And, as the one man adequate to the deed of perfect obedience, he offers us up to God. We are already given to God. It remains for us to ratify the gift and accept the forgiveness.

The cross reveals also, as nothing else could reveal, that God will stop at nothing in his love. In Christ he threw himself directly into human history, misery, and agony. He has taken his place beside us, and by his own act of ultimate commitment to us he releases and makes available a new power, enabling anyone who accepts God in Christ to be changed within and to center his being in God.

One thing more needs to be said about Christ. He did not stay dead. Crucified on a Friday, he was alive again that Sunday morning. He was seen by great numbers of his disciples, at widely scattered points, during a period of more than a month, before he bade them farewell and returned to his Father in heaven. But his departure did not mean that they had lost him. Once he was present with small groups of people in Palestine. Now he is available and present everywhere, whenever he meets the response of faith.

Any attempt to put all this into words is doomed to failure. Words are too cold, too halting. Theology itself is only a series of footnotes, useful but secondary. The primary thing is what has happened and still happens. Man, God, and love come together in one man. Through him we find God, learn love, and discover for the first time what the living "I" within us is.

Appendix A

THE MAJOR HURDLES

THE STUDENT COMMENTS ON RELIGION, INTERSPERSED throughout this book, are all authentic. I have quietly normalized the spelling and punctuation, but resisted the temptation to do any extensive surgery.

These comments were garnered from unsigned themes written in a number of my English classes over a period of several years. Slightly fewer than one hundred papers accumulated in all—obviously not enough for any important statistical conclusions, but sufficient to give me a fair idea of what are the major hurdles on the road to Christianity, as my students see it.

Conversations with students on other campuses have convinced me that the questions which are most frequently mentioned at Beloit College are those talked about elsewhere. So, for the benefit of anyone curious to see the results of this tiny sampling, I have listed the nine stumbling blocks mentioned in as many as one-tenth of the themes, with the percentage of writers naming them; but too much importance should not be attached to the list, in view of the small number of students involved.

Each student was allowed to choose between two subjects:

"Why I Hesitate to Be a Christian" and "Why Some of My Friends Hesitate to Be Christians." A few more than half chose the first topic. Here is the list:

Science versus religion	26 per cent
Ignorance ("I don't know enough about Christianity to make up my mind")	21
Christians ("People in the churches are a poor advertisement for Christianity")	17
The afterlife	17
Relativism ("It's all in the way you look at it")	17
The divinity of Christ	13
The problem of evil	12
Puritanism ("If you're a Christian you can't have any fun")	10
Changing times ("Christianity is old stuff")	10

Other stumbling blocks frequently mentioned: the historicity of the Bible, the question of miracles, and the charge that Christianity is either too vague or too dogmatic. (Evidently it depends on the kind of Christianity you have been exposed to!)

The students who wrote these themes were left free to define Christianity as they wished. Had a particular definition been given in advance (for example, the phrasing used by the World Council of Churches: faith in Christ as "God and Saviour"), the percentage for hurdle number 6 (the divinity of Christ) would undoubtedly have jumped, and a number of students would have shifted from topic 2 to topic 1—"Why *I* Hesitate to Be a Christian."

Another factor is of some importance. Beloit is a college with a long-standing, though nondenominational, Christian tradition. Conditions for the most part work toward making a religious commitment relatively easy. On many campuses of a more secular type I suspect that a questionnaire would reveal a much grimmer and glummer picture.

Appendix B

BOOKS FOR FURTHER READING

BASIC CHRISTIANITY

G. B. Caird, *The Truth of the Gospel* (Oxford University Press, New York, 1950).

Henry P. Van Dusen, *Life's Meaning* (Association Press, New York, 1951).

C. S. Lewis, *The Case for Christianity, Beyond Personality*, and *Christian Behaviour* (Macmillan Company, New York, 1943, 1945, 1944).

John S. Whale, *Christian Doctrine* (Cambridge University Press, New York, 1941).

Bernard I. Bell, *Beyond Agnosticism* (Harper & Brothers, New York, 1929).

Karl Barth, *Dogmatics in Outline* (Philosophical Library, New York, 1949).

THE EVIDENCE FOR CHRISTIANITY

Alan Richardson, *The Gospel and Modern Thought* (Oxford University Press, New York, 1950).

C. S. Lewis, *The Case for Christianity*.

G. B. Caird, *The Truth of the Gospel*.

FRANK HANFT, *You Can Believe: A Lawyer's Brief for Christianity* (Bobbs-Merrill Company, Indianapolis, 1952).

DOROTHY L. SAYERS, *The Mind of the Maker* (Harcourt, Brace & Company, New York, 1942). An interpretation of the Trinity, based on the analogy with the creative process.

FRANK MORISON (i.e., ALBERT H. ROSS), *Who Moved the Stone?* (6th ed., Zondervan Publishing House, Grand Rapids, Mich.). The evidence for the Resurrection.

THE LIFE OF CHRIST

HENRY M. BATTENHOUSE, *Christ in the Gospels* (Ronald Press Company, New York, 1952). Includes an excellent discussion of recent New Testament scholarship.

ALBERT T. OLMSTEAD, *Jesus in the Light of History* (Charles Scribner's Sons, New York, 1942).

WILLARD L. SPERRY, *Jesus Then and Now* (Harper & Brothers, New York, 1949).

ARCHIBALD M. HUNTER, *The Work and Words of Jesus* (Westminster Press, Philadelphia, 1950). Somewhat technical, but very meaty.

DOROTHY L. SAYERS, *The Man Born to Be King* (Harper & Brothers, New York, 1949). A brilliant series of radio plays on the life of Christ, written in the language of today.

GIOVANNI PAPINI, *Life of Christ*, translated by Dorothy Canfield Fisher (Harcourt, Brace & Company, New York, 1923).

GREVILLE COOKE, *The Light of the World* (Bobbs-Merrill Company, Indianapolis, 1950).

THE BIBLE

The King James version remains the most beautiful and majestic of all English translations, but its language is so archaic as to be frequently obscure and sometimes positively misleading. Anyone concerned with reading the Bible for its message as well as its beauty should possess one of the more modern translations. Several excellent versions have been prepared in recent years by individuals: Moffatt, Knox, etc. A very colloquial translation is available in the Smith-Goodspeed version, *The Complete Bible: An American Translation* (University of Chicago Press, Chicago, 1939). A newer version by a committee of outstanding scholars, preserving much of the literary quality of the King James translation, is the Revised Standard Version (Thomas Nelson & Sons, New York, 1952).

A good abridgment of the King James Bible, with a short, clear commentary for each section, is *The Shorter Oxford Bible*, ed. G. W. Briggs *et al.* (Oxford University Press, New York, 1951).

J. B. Phillips has made a very free and powerful translation of the New Testament Epistles and Gospels in *Letters to Young Churches* and *The Gospels Translated into Modern English* (Macmillan Company, New York, 1947, 1953).

A number of helpful guides to the Bible are available, including: EDGAR J. GOODSPEED, *How to Read the Bible* (John C. Winston Company, Philadelphia, 1946), C. H. DODD, *About the Gospels* (Cambridge University Press, New York, 1950), and MARY ELLEN CHASE, *The Bible and the Common Reader* (rev. ed., Macmillan Company, 1952).

PRAYER

THOMAS R. KELLY, *A Testament of Devotion* (Harper & Brothers, New York, 1941).

CONSTANCE GARRETT, *Growth in Prayer* (Macmillan Company, New York, 1950).

LYNN JAMES RADCLIFFE, *Making Prayer Real* (Abingdon-Cokesbury Press, New York, 1952).

CARROLL E. SIMCOX, *Living the Lord's Prayer* (Morehouse-Gorham Company, New York, 1951).

GEORGE A. BUTTRICK, *Prayer* (Abingdon-Cokesbury Press, New York, Nashville, 1942).

MIRACLES AND THE SUPERNATURAL

C. S. LEWIS, *Miracles* (Macmillan Company, New York, 1947). A very clear, philosophic treatment of the whole question of the supernatural.

AGNES SANFORD, *The Healing Light* (Macalester Park Publishing

Company, St. Paul, Minn., 1949). This and the next book deal with spiritual healing.

REBECCA BEARD, *Everyman's Search* (Merrybrook Press, Wells, Vt., 1950).

THE CHRISTIAN IDEA OF LOVE

Several novelists have succeeded better here than most of the theologians. Some of the best examples:

ALAN PATON, *Cry, the Beloved Country* (Charles Scribner's Sons, New York, 1948).

FËDOR DOSTOEVSKI, *Crime and Punishment* (various publishers).

CHARLES WILLIAMS, *Descent into Hell* and *All Hallows' Eve* (Pellegrini & Cudahy, New York, 1949, 1948).

THE HISTORY OF THE CHURCH

R. W. MOORE, *The Furtherance of the Gospel* (Oxford University Press, New York, 1950).

CHARLES WILLIAMS, *The Descent of the Dove* (new ed., Pellegrini & Cudahy, New York, 1950).

WILLISTON WALKER, *A History of the Christian Church* (Charles Scribner's Sons, New York, 1918).

THE CHARACTERISTICS OF DIFFERENT DENOMINATIONS

J. PAUL WILLIAMS, *What Americans Believe and How They Worship* (Harper & Brothers, New York, 1952).

CHRISTIANITY AND SOCIETY

H. RICHARD NIEBUHR, *Christ and Culture* (Harper & Brothers, New York, 1951).

ELTON TRUEBLOOD, *The Life We Prize* (Harper & Brothers, New York, 1951).

CHAD WALSH, *Early Christians of the 21st Century* (Harper & Brothers, New York, 1950).

CHARLES W. LOWRY, *Communism and Christ* (Morehouse-Gorham Company, New York, 1952).

To this list one could add practically all of Reinhold Niebuhr's books. He is equally profound as a religious and social thinker.

SCIENCE AND RELIGION

DANIEL LUZON MORRIS, *Possibilities Unlimited* (Harper & Brothers, New York, 1952).

D. R. G. OWEN, *Scientism, Man, and Religion* (Westminster Press, Philadelphia, 1952).

ANTHONY STANDEN, *Science Is a Sacred Cow* (E. P. Dutton & Company, New York, 1950).

JOHN BAILLIE, *Natural Science and the Spiritual Life* (Charles Scribner's Sons, New York, 1952). Very short, very tightly packed; a good philosophic work-out.

PIERRE LECOMTE DU NOÜY, *Human Destiny* (Longmans, Green & Company, New York, 1947, and New American Library of World Literature, New York). The theistic implications of Evolution.

GORDON WILLARD ALLPORT, *The Individual and His Religion: A Psychological Interpretation* (Macmillan Company, New York, 1950).

LAURENCE W. GRENSTED, *The Psychology of Religion* (Oxford University Press, New York, 1952).

RELATIVISM AND NATURAL LAW

C. S. LEWIS, *The Abolition of Man* (Macmillan Company, New York, 1947).

A. CAMPBELL GARNETT, *The Moral Nature of Man* (Ronald Press Company, New York, 1952).

W

1126-90

N